THE

GARDEN

IN

AUTUMN

HENRY HOLT AND COMPANY ❧ NEW YORK

THE

GARDEN

IN

AUTUMN

by Allen Lacy

Henry Holt and Company, Inc.
Publishers since 1866
115 West 18th Street
New York, New York 10011

Henry Holt ® is a registered
trademark of Henry Holt and Company, Inc.

Published in Canada by Fitzhenry & Whiteside Ltd.,
195 Allstate Parkway, Markham, Ontario L3R 4T8.

Excerpt from *Gardens in Winter* by Elizabeth Lawrence
copyright © 1961 by Elizabeth Lawrence;
reprinted by permission of Harper & Row Publishers, Inc.
Excerpt from *Lob's Wood* by Elizabeth Lawrence
copyright © 1971 by Elizabeth Lawrence;
reprinted by permission of Miss Lawrence's estate.

Library of Congress Catalog Card Number: 95-79212

ISBN 0-8050-4067-6

Henry Holt books are available for special promotions
and premiums. For details contact: Director, Special Markets.

First published in hardcover in 1990
by The Atlantic Monthly Press.

First Owl Book Edition—1995

Design by Julie Duquet

Printed in the United States of America
All first editions are printed on acid-free paper.∞

10 9 8 7 6 5 4 3 2 1

For Allen, Ann, Edith, J.C., Joanne, and Nancy

Contents

Preface

Writing is often thought to be a solitary pursuit, and perhaps it is for the novelist or the poet. But writing about gardening is gregarious and social. It is the product of a long and ongoing conversation, and it involves much more listening than speaking. Some of the parties to my own conversation about gardening, which began when I was growing up in Texas in a family of gardeners, no longer walk this earth. They include those who have written enduring books on gardening—Celia Thaxter, Richardson Wright, Louise Beebe Wilder, Vita Sackville-West, Elizabeth Lawrence, and many others in a great communion of saints. Some participants in this continuing conversation are my contemporaries, friends from all across the United States. In writing about gardening, I have always sought to observe plants directly and personally, but friendship has ever been essential. Hardly a day goes by without at least one telephone call to or from someone in another part of the country about plants and gardening. The letter carrier often brings mail reporting on such weighty matters as the spectacular bloom this year on *Crambe cordifolia* or the remarkable qualities of lablab beans climbing a trellis in a friend's garden; letter writing may be moribund in the world today, but it still flourishes among gardeners. And in early spring and the middle days of fall, UPS brings packages from friends eager to share this uncommon monkshood or that unusual sedum, just as I send them seeds of Scotch thistles or an unusual aquilegia they may not yet have grown. The exchange of ideas is endless. These friends and their ideas are an inextricable part of this book: it probably would not have been written without them. They are often quoted or cited by name, but even where they are not, there is scarcely a page where they are absent.

A WORD IS in order about the origins of *The Garden in Autumn.* In September of 1988, I was suddenly struck by the accumulated evidence in my own garden that autumn could be the very best of seasons. The thought immediately occurred to me that I had never seen a book on the autumn garden, although the topic is necessarily touched on in a great number of books that follow the entire sequence of the gardening year. Checking this vague impression with my friend Elisabeth Woodburn, whose Booknoll Farm is the best source of classic horticultural texts in the country, and with Paulette Rickert of Capability's Books, whose catalogue lists over eight hundred contemporary titles on gardening, I discovered that my hunch was correct: there was a void in our gardening literature.

No writer loves anything more than a void, so I started to work—with, as the Beatles put it, a little help from my friends. From the East Coast and the West, from North and South, they wrote or telephoned offering suggestions, reports on the events in their gardens, and detailed observations about plants they found especially wonderful at this time of year. This book owes much to many people: Ann Blomberg, Fred Godomski, Kim Hawks, Allen

and Robbie Jones, Beverly Lowry, Margaret Marsh, Penelope May-
nard, Lynden B. Miller, Stephen Lacey, Allen Paterson, Pat Stra-
chan, Frances Tenenbaum, Andre Viette, Hannah Withers, and
Linda Yang have all made contributions for which I am grateful.
They, as well as a host of plants and my wife Hella and our two
sons, Paul and Michael, are part of my cast of characters. Hella,
I think, deserves a medal for patience. Few writers are easy to live
with, and I know that while in the grip of an intense period of
writing—and of rewriting—I was not. My autumn garden, furthermore, is her autumn garden, and I am fully aware of the situational
irony that when I am writing about gardening it is Hella who is
outdoors, involved in the pursuit.

But some other friends gave such outstanding support that I
dedicate the book to them. Allen Bush, the owner of Holbrook
Farm and Nursery in Fletcher, North Carolina, was generous with
plants, advice, and a willing ear in many long telephone conversa-
tions. Edith Eddleman, a garden designer, also in North Carolina,
who is the curator of the exemplary herbaceous border at the North
Carolina State University Arboretum in Raleigh, provided much
help, especially regarding native North American perennials.
Joanne Ferguson, to whom I owe the treasured opportunity of
editing Elizabeth Lawrence's *Gardening for Love: The Market Bulle-
tins* for Duke University Press, where she is editor-in-chief, read
every draft of this book and offered many a valuable suggestion.
Nancy Goodwin, the owner of Montrose Nursery in Hillsborough,
North Carolina, which is among the very best sources of unusual
perennials in the country, took time from a busy shipping season
to write long letters over the course of an entire autumn and never
failed to answer the telephone when I called with a question. Ann
Lovejoy, the author of *The Year in Bloom*, a wonderful collection
of personal essays on gardening, similarly reported on the events
in her own fine garden on an island in Puget Sound, providing
something of a West Coast perspective. Dr. J. C. Raulston, professor of horticulture at North Carolina State University and director
of its arboretum, gave much good counsel on the woody plants that
are his special love, although I suspect he might wish that I had
paid them greater attention instead of dwelling so much on the

perennials that figure largely in my own affections. All six of these
friends offered many a valuable suggestion for the book's improvement.

I also owe special thanks to my agent, Helen Pratt, who gave
constant encouragement all along the way, and to my editor, John
Barstow. John was for three years my editor at *Horticulture* magazine, and I am delighted that he is my editor still. His enthusiasm
for the topic of autumn gardens kept me going during a long period
of revision. Very few writers today can claim the same degree of
editorial judgment and attention that he provided. I also claim him
proudly as a member of a circle of good friends who are bound
together by their affection for plants and gardens.

It was not my intent to be encyclopedic, nor do I claim that this
book is the final word on gardens in autumn. It is written instead
out of my own experience to date, buttressed by the experiences of
good friends. The great majority of plants that are discussed I have
either grown or seen and admired in gardens other than my own.
And this book reflects my experience in another way. I am a
Southerner—born and bred and raised—who has lived half his life
north of the Mason-Dixon line. I have gardened in southern New
Jersey for the past seventeen years, but before that I lived and
planted gardens in Texas, North Carolina, Virginia, and upstate
New York. Experience has taught me that "hardiness" has different meanings in different parts of the country. In the Northeast
and Midwest, winter hardiness is the main concern—the ability of
a plant (or its roots) to survive a range of average minimum winter
temperatures expressed in the United States Department of Agriculture's well-known system of climatic zones. Gardeners in the
Upper and Middle South are necessarily concerned with winter
hardiness as well, but they recognize that summer hardiness—the
ability of a plant to survive prolonged periods of heat and the hot
and humid still nights that promote fungal diseases and other
maladies—is also critical. It is impossible to write a book on
gardening that is universal. Everyone gardens in the highly particular, on one spot of home ground at the intersection of this degree
of latitude and that degree of longitude.

The Spanish philosopher Miguel de Unamuno put the matter

neatly: the universal is the particular and the concrete, not the abstract or the general. What I have learned about gardening over the past seventeen years, I have learned on a corner lot on a busy thoroughfare that starts off as Main Street three towns to the north but changes to Shore Road before it reaches us. I live in the middle reaches of Zone 7, the transition between North and South. Here gray birches reach the southernmost extent of their range. *Magnolia grandiflora* and camellias will survive here, but just barely, and the magnolias remain small trees, not achieving the towering heights they reach in Virginia and states to its south. Summers are hot here, if tempered somewhat by breezes from the Atlantic Ocean, which lies about four miles from my front door. Winters can be as fierce as they are in Springfield, Massachusetts, or Binghamton, New York, but they lack the benefit that a dependable covering of snow offers plants during the coldest months. The soil that I dig in is sandy—a joy to work, or at least not as difficult as the black clay I grew up with in Texas. But sandy soil is also quick to dry out during times of high winds or high temperatures.

I might mention that when we moved here almost two decades ago, having bought a former farmhouse built in 1812 that is now surrounded by suburbia, there was no garden. There was much grass to mow, few trees or shrubs, and an unimpeded view from the street of seven neighboring houses. Now those houses cannot be seen either from the street or from my garden, because there is a thicket of ornamental grasses, bamboos, and shrubs and small trees all along the periphery of our lot. The garden came into being not as a result of thoughtful design, but from long practice in acquiring as many interesting plants as possible and packing them into as little space as possible, with special attention in recent years to the plants of the late season and autumn. I write here about these plants. Not all of them will thrive everywhere, but many will, and my main purpose is to encourage fellow gardeners to pay attention to the neglected but glorious possibilities of the fall garden.

The Neglected Season

About autumn and gardens, in the horticultural version of what John Kenneth Galbraith called the conventional wisdom, there is a peculiar and widespread notion that spring and summer are the gardening seasons, and that autumn brings everything to an end, except for chrysanthemums. Autumn means watching the leaves turn briefly vivid in the woods and on hillsides, and it means listening to the roar of the crowds and the blare of the marching bands at a Saturday afternoon football game at the high school a couple of blocks away. It is the time when geese honk overhead as they migrate south in search of food and a gentle winter climate. It is the time of pumpkins ripening in the fields and then of jack-o-lanterns on front porches. For gardeners, however, autumn is all too often little more than a season of chores. We must rake our leaves and haul them to the compost heap. We must tidy up the perennial beds and cut back annuals as they blacken with frost. We must kneel down in the dirt and plant the crocuses and daffodils and tulips that will brighten our spirits in spring. We must clean and oil our hoes and sharpen our pruning shears and put them away in shed or garage until their time comes round again. Autumn marks the end of the gardening year.

For too many of us, everything that I have said holds true. Our autumn gardens look sad and forlorn while we labor with the chores. But it need not be so at all. Many of us have learned to be springtime and summertime gardeners only, paying almost no heed to fall. We may, with somewhat greater difficulty, learn to be autumn gardeners as well. A garden can be at its very best in autumn—a proposition I mean to demonstrate by exploring the plants of autumn. Certainly, in most of America, the best time to be in the garden is in the fall, even if it's only to do the chores. It is a kindly season, and a forgiving one, with its own special rhythms. Although the nights grow steadily cooler and longer, the soil cools down more gradually, still holding summer hostage. It warms our hands and our souls as we work in it. The summer may have been humid and sweltering, but in autumn it becomes a pleasure to go outside and work. There may be some chilly days, and even on warm ones a passing cloud may momentarily come between us and the sun, but when it moves on and the sun's rays strike our cheeks once again, summer returns, except that the heat is much more welcome than it was in July.

The sense of rush and urgency that we felt in gardening last spring is absent now. In the spring, the gardener hastens from one chore to another, with little time to sit back and enjoy the garden. If orders of perennials already in active growth come by mail or UPS from six different nurseries on the same Friday in April, they must be planted immediately or risk being lost. Perennials that arrive on the doorstep in the autumn, near their time of dormancy, can be treated with less frenzy—and with more time to consider their best location. Procrastination that would be fatal in the spring is permissible in the fall.

Autumn is in fact the best season of the year to transplant many perennials and woody plants. They have time to form new roots and make themselves at home. Soil that is still warm, plus the slow, soft rains typical of autumn in much of the country, encourage strong root growth. Cool nights discourage sappy vegetative growth that can be damaged by the more extreme weather to come. Fall-planted perennials and shrubs will not suffer the stress that afflicts some of those planted in spring as they struggle to make root systems and also come into flower in too brief a time. This rule about planting in autumn, like all good rules, has its notable exceptions. Fall is not a good time for dividing and transplanting members of the compositae, or daisy, family, particularly those that have evergreen tendencies, like Shasta daisies, gaillardia, and coreopsis.

Autumn is a time of sweet disorder and permissible procrastination.

Perennials that are a bit on the tender side to begin with, such as geum, some of the campanulas, and *Ceratostigma plumbaginoides,* should be held off till spring. There is good reason, furthermore, to keep hands off any plant of intrinsic winter interest, such as the great number of ornamental grasses and many of the sedums and astilbes and other plants with attractive, long-lasting seed heads. Nevertheless it's obvious that a great number of plants are left that are ideal for fall transplanting—daylilies, hostas, meadow rues, heucheras, and on down a long list.

Even weeding becomes a pleasure in autumn, or at least it seems less of a drudgery. If the garden has been reasonably well tended earlier in the year, the few weeds that remain are easily dispatched. The growth of the weeds of late spring and summer has slowed, and there is no longer that horrendous shock of late May—

The aptly named *Boltonia aster-oides* 'Snowbank' in its early fall profusion. In my garden, it puts on this show for about two weeks, starting in early September.

pulling up every weed in sight and then discovering a lusty new crop of enemies four days later. A few pieces of crab grass will have survived in odd corners here and there, of course, also purslane, but these and other stray summer weeds occasion no backaches to remove. In autumn, to be sure, the winter weeds appear, chickweed and dandelions and the rest, but they are slow starters. They bide their time, so I can bide mine. There's an unstable peace between us, almost an attitude of live-and-let-live.

Thus far, I have stayed with the more obvious advantages of late-season gardening, reflections on autumn by a spring and summer gardener grateful for the lull among weeds, ready to kneel down and plant my spring bulbs, writing what I could have written a decade ago and would have written then. But some Septembers ago, I noticed that something had happened in my garden, a shifting of balance by small accretions that tilted the plot of land I till toward autumn. Gradually, a couple of plants at a time and without deliberate intent, I had accumulated perennials and shrubs with a prolonged period of bloom, plants whose flowers lingered well into fall, as well as those, like asters, whose flowers first appeared in autumn. It was these plants themselves that taught me about the overlooked possibilities of the season. Once I had learned their lesson, I began seeking out additional plants for an autumn garden. I took full advantage of the great and growing number of fine mail-order nurseries in America—some of them large and well known, others quite small, often run by only one or two people— which offer plants not available at local garden centers. Garden centers have their place, but almost all of their customers live close at hand, usually within a twenty-five-mile radius or less, and they usually want the standard kind of plants that typify a suburban neighborhood. A mail-order nursery, on the other hand, serves an entire nation, and its customers may well be athirst for uncommon plants, including those that are suitable for the autumn garden.

Thanks largely to these specialized nurseries, my own garden has come to be at its best in the fall, with a wealth of bloom I could not have imagined just five years ago. On a recent day in mid-September I counted some seventy-five different kinds of perennials, annuals, shrubs, and bulbs in bloom, in a long list from abelia

'Edward Goucher' to viola 'Molly Sanderson'. A good many other plants were not in bloom yet, but started to bloom later on. These, mostly October bloomers, included *Chrysanthemum nipponicum, C. arcticum,* various hardy cyclamens, two perennial sunflowers, *Lespedeza thunbergii,* or Japanese bush clover, and five different cultivars of the *x* darleyensis winter heaths—all by themselves a substantial group of worthy plants. Five weeks later, only seventeen of the mid-September seventy-five had quit blooming for the year. Some eleven were near quitting. All the rest were still putting on a show. Even on Thanksgiving, the garden had not put in its final word. The bracts of salvia 'Indigo Spires' were still good for bouquets, even if the foliage had turned to mush in a black freeze. Some chrysanthemums remained. A clump of pink oxalis continued the bloom it had started in May, although on cold, cloudy days the blossoms remained closed. Two white herbaceous potentillas, usually spring bloomers, were in flower—either untypically early or untypically late, I couldn't say which. Sweet alyssum still bloomed, as did abelia and 'Betty Prior' roses. Deep blue and apricot primroses—the apricot one deeply honeyed—blossomed by a doorstep, and a volunteer Johnny-jump-up with unusually large deep purple blossoms had just chimed in.

There is an unmistakable rhythm in the gardening year. With the coming of early spring, the garden moves from sparse bloom into the explosive profusion of midsummer. The movement from this midsummer bounty of bloom toward winter reverses the cycle, turning it back toward sparseness. Autumn inevitably is a season of winding down, of ceasing, but its changes are very slow and gradual, and if plants are chosen carefully for what they bring to the garden at this time of year, fall can also bring bounty—and I don't mean only its harvest of apples and pumpkins. The same year that I made those three successive inventories of what was blooming from the middle of September to Thanksgiving, I made a late April inventory as well. It showed thirty-nine different kinds of plants in bloom. Some, like tulips and crown imperials, were highly spectacular. But the inventory itself was less rich and various than its equivalent in the middle of October. The problem with our gardens in autumn lies not in the absence of plants that are lovely

then but in our neglect of the season, our failure to widen our knowledge and exercise our imaginations, and our sticking to old, well-trodden, and familiar paths.

IF AUTUMN CAN be the best season in the gardening year, given some careful attention to choosing plants, the question naturally arises: why have we paid it so little heed? There are three possible answers.

One answer, surely, is the fall display of color in our woodlands. With oaks and maples and birches and tupelos putting on their blowtorch spectacle, our eyes and our thoughts are focused on Nature, in uppercase, and diverted from that part of the natural

Evidence of the splendor that can adorn the perennial border in September. Here, next to the erect spikes of perennial salvias, the billowing dusty-pink flower clusters of Joe Pye weed echo the pure white panicles of phlox 'Miss Lingard', with dahlia 'Japanese Bishop', *Helenium* 'Moorheim Beauty', and *Rudbeckia nitida* 'Herbstsonne' as a backdrop.

order we make and contrive in our home plots. And there is no question about it: the autumnal foliage in North America is unmatched elsewhere on earth. In his "Essay on American Scenery," published in *The Atlantic Monthly* in 1836, the landscape painter Thomas Cole put it well:

> There is one season when the American forest surpasses all the world in gorgeousness—that is the autumnal:—then every hill and dale is riant in the luxury of color—every hue is there, from the liveliest green to deepest purple—from the most golden yellow to the intensest crimson. The artist looks despairingly upon this glowing landscape, and in the old world his truest imitations of the American forest, at this season, are called falsely bright, and scenes in fairy land.

We can hardly ignore the conflagration of color overhead and on distant hillsides, nor should we. But neither should we ignore the equally real if less flamboyant beauties that, if we plan for them, we may have much closer at hand, in our gardens. We are also, I think, often deceived about autumn color. Autumn, conventional thinking has it, is the season of flame and fire and incandescence, of scarlet and crimson and bright gold. Indeed, all these colors are present, and so insistently that only a clod could fail to notice them. But the palette of autumn also embraces more subtle tones and shades. The lowly and despised crab grass turns to a fine haze of mauve-pink as it goes to seed where it has been allowed to grow unchecked. To name the colors of autumn is to speak of lavender and lilac and buff rose, and finally to give up the effort, since at this season of the year there are so many colors with no names in any language.

Another reason that we pay less attention to the possibilities of the autumn garden is that the season is imprisoned in a system of easy but misleading metaphors. The year has its seasons, we say, and so does a human life. Spring is rebirth and youth. Summer is the vigorous time when we exercise the physical and mental powers of adulthood. Winter is death, and so autumn must of course be

Dionysus, ancient god of wine and the waning year, still lives in many gardens. Here he appears with a sacrificial offering of ripe grapes, as well as the stone ones in his hair.

senescence, a transition from life to death, a dying season cheered
only by the final hurrahs of the maples and sweet gums. The
language of death enters our autumn vocabularies in many ways.
We speak of a "killing freeze," which may be defined as the first
frost that blasts the foliage of perennial salvias. (Impatiens will
already have been taken out by light frosts that are inconsequential
for most other plants.) But "killing" is, again, a metaphorical term,
and it is misleading. Far more plants survive frost than die. Woody
plants are seldom touched, except in extraordinary circumstances
like the bitter freeze that hit much of the South in December 1983
on the heels of an unusually mild fall that left many crape myrtles
and boxwoods still in active growth. Only the tenderest kinds of
annuals die when the temperature drops below 32 degrees, and
even these may survive for a time if they are in a protected spot.
Some annuals, such as pelargoniums and petunias, shrug off what
is technically a killing freeze, maintaining green foliage and keeping up bloom until temperatures drop well into the 20s for several
days. Other annuals grow and even blossom throughout the winter,
chickweed being the most common example.

The killing freeze is not an executioner's ax. And leaf-fall is
only in part an ending, for when it occurs it reveals a host of
beginnings. Azaleas, dogwoods, and rhododendrons already bear
fat buds that will flower next spring. The catkins on a male hazelnut
begin their slow elongation, a process that will continue throughout
winter. Bare of foliage, paulownia trees display clusters of the
spring flower buds to come, equally prominent with the clusters of
seed pods that have ripened but will not open until the middle of
the following summer. Nor is a killing freeze—or even several of
them—an absolute point of demarcation. A few roses may bloom
almost to Christmas, even in the chilly upper reaches of Zone 7.
The perennials that die back (a slightly different use of the meta-
phor) lose only part of this year's growth. Many of them, such as
heleniums and Shasta daisies, have produced rosettes of new foliage that will stay fresh and green all winter long. Others, like
perennial asters and certain of the helianthuses, send out fat, pale
ivory underground shoots well before their last flower fades and
their leaves turn first yellow and then brown. Summer dormancy

broken, fresh leaves have already appeared on Madonna lilies,
grape hyacinths, and Oriental poppies.

A final reason we have paid too little attention to the possibilities of the autumn garden is probably that we base so many of our expectations on the rich horticultural traditions of Great Britain and on its accompanying literature. We have learned much from the English, and we will no doubt continue to learn, as America begins to become a nation of gardeners that will in time rival Britain. But England is, by necessity, as we shall see, a nation of spring and summer gardeners. English gardens have very little to teach us about fall.

Summer, to begin with, is a temperate and congenial season in Great Britain, while in much of the United States it is fiercely unpleasant for weeks or even months on end. Here's part of a letter written to me one October by the novelist Beverly Lowry, who lives in San Marcos, Texas:

> This summer, by August, I decided to think as if I were in Vermont and this was January, and the snow had blizzarded against the window. I stayed inside in the air conditioning, went out only when I had to and when I did walked slowly and carefully. The lawn died. My silver-leafed thyme keeled over. I could not water the sage or the impatiens enough. Eventually I let the impatiens die. They were leggy anyway, but mainly I just could not keep up. If I was gone a couple of nights and the house sitter neglected them, they went limp. Like cats when you go away, they gave me nasty looks—more, I thought, than I deserved. So—cruel stepmother—I let them die.

Since I was born and raised in Texas (before the advent of air conditioning anywhere except in picture-show palaces), I can testify to the truth of Beverly's remarks. The miseries of a Texas summer for both people and plants are deep in my experience. I remember the annual rite in May of rolling up wool carpets and storing them in the attic, since bare wooden floors were cooler. I remember the weeks and weeks of blast-furnace weather, the chores tended to at dawn or near nightfall to escape the bright hot sun, the nights when it never really cooled down, the ice cubes to suck on, and the huge pitchers of iced tea with mint and lemon slices. I remember, too, the deep cracks that appeared in our black clay as it dried up, the wilted and stunted annuals, the rains that didn't come until long after they were needed.

Texas, of course, has no monopoly on torrid summer weather, but everywhere in the country autumn brings recompense for summer. More from Beverly Lowry:

> Here, as you well know, fall really is the great season. The relief people feel after a long hard winter is what we go through down here after the same kind of summer. Finally, we and the plants are getting a break. And finally we feel the urge simply to go out there again and work and play.

Recompense means that our suffering in summer is made up for by the pleasure and joy that we can find in autumn. But it means something else as well. If we envy the English their mild summers and the plants they can grow then that we cannot, then they must envy us our autumns and the plants we can grow then that they cannot. The British writer Christopher Lloyd wondered, in an article in *Horticulture* a few years ago, why Americans fret so much about plants we cannot grow well instead of cherishing ones we can grow that he cannot in his garden in Sussex. And one November another British writer, Stephen Lacey, wrote in a letter after he had toured the northeastern American lecture circuit in October:

> Over here, autumn is generally marked by the collapse of the herbaceous border and the start of winter blooming shrubs rather than by a bonfire of brilliant foliage. The problem is that we do not see much of that crisp, sunny weather that you enjoy at this time of year; steady drizzle, chilly winds, and gray overcast skies are the norm for us, so there is little temptation to linger outdoors. But there are horticultural reasons for the lack of autumn spectacle in British gardens. The season has not been preceded by a

long, hot summer. This means that many of the plants which are mainstays in American gardens never have a chance to ripen over here. I saw an array of fruits, berries, flowers, and seedheads in the U.S. which I hadn't seen here even though the plants are common in Britain. Oh, if only my Miscanthus would produce those red plumes!

In England, Lacey says, among ornamental grasses only the "ubiquitous pampas grasses" can be counted on to flower, bringing their touch of drama and grace to the landscape in autumn and then into winter. And between them, Lowry and Lacey put the matter neatly: in Texas, no one feels like going outside in the summer; in England, in the fall.

I find it instructive, in comparing autumn in Great Britain with our own experience of the season, to look at some literary sources. British nature poets, on comfortable and lyrical ground with spring and summer, turn dour and unenthusiastic when autumn is the topic. Keats, in his ode "To Autumn," comes up with little besides mists, crickets, apples, and swelling gourds as tokens of fall. He also writes that

> *Then in a wailful choir the small gnats mourn*
> *Among the river sallows, borne aloft*
> *Or sinking as the light wind lives or dies. . . .*

Thomas Hood's "Ode: Autumn" mentions owls, mossy elms, departed swallows, dead roses, bitter fruits, and a cloudy prison for the soul, and it begins with a general tone of pessimism and despair:

> *I saw old Autumn in the misty morn*
> *Stand shadowless like Silence, listening*
> *To silence, for no lonely bird would sing*
> *Into his hollow ear from woods forlorn. . . .*

Nor were these Hood's final words on the subject. During his short life between 1799 and 1845, this British romantic poet made

something of a career of bashing the season every chance he got.
His poem titled simply "No" concludes as follows:

> *No warmth, no cheerfulness, no healthful ease,*
> *No comfortable feel in any member—*
> *No shade, no shine, no butterflies, no bees,*
> *No fruits, no flowers, no leaves, no birds—*
> *November!*

Tennyson was equally lugubrious in his poem "Song":

> *The air is damp and hushed and close,*
> *As a sick man's room when he taketh repose*
> *An hour before death—*
> *My very heart faints and the whole soul grieves*
> *At the moist rich smell of the rotting leaves,*
> *And the breath*
> *Of the fading edges of box beneath,*
> *And the year's last rose.*

Alexander Pope's Third Pastoral, "Autumn," dispenses similarly
gloomy thoughts:

> *Ye flowers that droop, forsaken by the spring,*
> *Ye birds that, left by summer, cease to sing,*
> *Ye trees that fade when autumn heats remove,*
> *Say, is not absence death to those who love.*

I scarcely need to quote Shelley on autumn, considering that he
titles one poem on the subject "A Dirge." But if British poetry
about autumn is dismal and cheerless, American poetry is, to the
contrary, strikingly sunny and bright. Thoreau was enamored of
the pleasures that fall brings:

> *The moon now rises to her absolute rule,*
> *And the husbandman and the hunter*

Acknowledge her for their mistress.
Asters and goldenrod reign in the fields
And the life everlasting withers not.
The fields are reaped and shorn of their pride
But an inward verdure still crowns them;
The thistle scatters its down on the pool
And yellow leaves clothe the river—
And nought disturbs the serious life of men.

And Emily Dickinson, writing about the native fringed gentian, a late bloomer often the victim of a sudden frost, shows no melancholy whatsoever, but only delight in its beauty—

But just before the snows
There came a purple creature
That ravished all the hill:
And summer hid her forehead,
And mockery was still.
The frosts were her condition:
The Tyrian would not come
Until the North evoked it,
"Creator! shall I bloom!"

Occasionally popular nineteenth-century American poets could wax melancholy about autumn, mourning it as a season of decay and loss. Both Celia Thaxter and William Cullen Bryant expressed this mood, but they seem to be following conventional English poetic themes, not quite putting their hearts into their elegiac words. In "Third of November" Bryant was far from bleak of spirit:

Glorious are the woods in their latest gold and crimson
. . . .
Such a kindly autumn, so mercifully dealing
With the growths of summer, I never yet have seen.

In "Evangeline," Henry Wadsworth Longfellow hailed autumn as "that beautiful season, the summer of All-Saints." Another popular American poet of the last century, Helen Hunt, wrote in "Asters and Golden Rod":

> *The lands are lit*
> *With all the autumn blaze of Golden Rod*
> *And everywhere the purple asters nod*
> *And bend and wave and flit.*

The differences between the poetry autumn has inspired in Great Britain and in America are not the product of differences in national character. They are founded, I believe, on scientific reality—a matter of latitude and the earth's tilt. Every part of the United States, except Alaska, lies well to the south of all of the British Isles. Our intuitive geography may place London due east of New York City, but our intuitive geography is out of whack. England lies east of Labrador. Its benevolent climate comes courtesy of the Gulf Stream, moderating what otherwise would be ferociously cold winters. Latitude, however, is absolute, and latitude governs the hours of daylight. The higher the degree of latitude north, the longer the summer day and the more prolonged the hours of twilight and dawn on either side of the summer solstice. The temperate English summers combined with the long hours of light enable British gardeners to plant herbaceous borders that are among the wonders of the horticultural world. But American gardeners gain an astronomical recompense when autumn arrives. Autumn not only repays us for the suffering we have endured in summer, but also offers us opportunities to make fall gardens such as our British counterparts can only imagine. Again, it is a matter of latitude. At the autumnal equinox in late September, the 21st or the 22nd or the 23rd, depending on the year, there is parity: Edinburgh and Savannah, Liverpool and San Francisco, Belfast and Dallas all have the same number of daylight hours, 12 hours and 4 minutes in a recent year. But right after the equinox, the light in the north begins to diminish, the less sharply the lower the latitude. On December 10, the sun rises in London (latitude 51° 30′ 00″ N) at 7:52 A.M. and sets at 3:53 P.M. In New York City (latitude 40° 45′ 06″ N), sunrise is at 7:09, sunset at 4:29. The differences

become even more dramatic if, say, Edinburgh and Atlanta are compared. Nor is the length of the day the only consideration. The jet stream, if it's behaving itself, descends in late September to English latitudes, bringing the nasty weather that it doesn't bring most of the United States until November. And finally, the lower position of the sun in England's skies in the autumn reduces the intensity of light, as do fog and mist.

Taken together, these matters of latitude, day length, and climate mean that if Americans are to learn to garden well in autumn, we must teach ourselves to take advantage of the relatively longer days, the clearer skies, and the greater intensity of light, that in our southerly location are a blessing to people and plants alike. We must go beyond the habits of mind that start and end with a few

In Lynden B. Miller's Connecticut garden, purple cabbages combine pleasingly with *Miscanthus sinensis* 'Variegatus' (center) and with the ripening leaves of Siberian irises and the variegated foliage of *Iris pallida* 'Variegata' (left). Blue oat grass *(Helictotrichon sempervirens)*, at right, completes the picture.

A rich tapestry of shrubs, perennials, and annuals can blanket the carefully planned autumn border. The distinctive textured leaves of oak-leaf hydrangea have turned rusty-red, consorting beautifully with one of the stars of the fall garden, *Anemone* 'September Charm'. Behind the anemones are the warm white blossoms of *Asteromoea mongolica*, a wonderful, trouble-free perennial saved by Elizabeth Lawrence, who noticed its merit and passed it along to nurserymen. Adding to the picture are (clockwise from lower left) the little pink buttons of the annual Centranthus, *Sedum* 'Autumn Joy', and the variegated leaves of *Cornus alba* 'Elegantissima'.

potted chrysanthemums to celebrate the season, seeking out the great wealth of neglected plants that together can make it a grand and varied feast.

In autumn, above every other season, it is possible to have a great harmony between the garden and the larger landscape of fields and meadows and roadsides. The plants of spring, by comparison, are welcome visitors from elsewhere on the planet. Most spring bulbs are from the Mediterranean basin. Flowering cherries and many other ornamental trees of spring hail from Asia. But in the autumn, the grasses and compositae that hold dominion in the American countryside have their garden equivalents. Indeed, in some cases, such as solidagos and eupatoriums, they may be not just equivalent but the same plants. I like to admire these handsome natives in my suburban garden and then be able to enjoy them along a roadside out in the country. I thus experience the countryside as something of a garden and experience my garden as a home for what has been only partially tamed.

We must also go beyond the notion that autumn is merely a time of tidying up the garden for the advent of winter and the hope of spring. One of the great charms of the fall season is its sweet disorder. Many of its best plants, from the August bloom of Joe Pye weed to the late October glory of the swamp sunflower, are tall and rangy, and they tend to lean a bit. One aster will drape itself over another, while other asters grow up through their neighbors, in a pleasant mingling. The plants of spring, in comparison, are mostly centered and separate. The autumn perennial border tends, in particular, toward tapestry, as the red stems of the tall seaside goldenrod lean into the more upright stems of the even taller tatar aster. The autumn garden becomes, to be honest, a little tatty around the edges. Slugs have long since had their way with the hostas, and leaf-miners with most species of aquilegia. Boltonia 'Snowbank' and aster 'Hella Lacy' refuse to sing a duet; the boltonia has put in its final note when the aster begins to sing.

Tidy souls who want their gardens always tidy may be tempted to resort to stakes, keeping every plant distinct from every other, or to shears, simply cutting plants to the ground when they show signs of waning. No one who knows me well could ever call me a tidy soul, and I am not fond of stakes, except in such extreme cases as *Salvia azurea* 'Grandiflora', a perennial four or five feet high which has such low ambitions that left unstaked it becomes a groundcover. What I love most about autumn is its layerings of one plant upon another or under another: the yellow needles of white pine that fall on the broad leaves of hostas as they go dormant, the strange fungi that spring up in the mulch around violets blooming one last time, the colchicums that emerge as a grand surprise amid carpets of periwinkle, the fresh and attractively marbled leaves of *Arum italicum* that unfold in October in shady, leaf-strewn corners and last right through winter's end. I also love, in midautumn, to plot spring, to push aside the dark green leaves of hellebores in order to stick in a few bulbs of lady tulips as a surprise for April. There is pleasure, of course, in tidying up—in raking leaves, in cutting back to the ground those perennials which hold no interest in winter, in hauling spent vegetation to the compost heap and its slow microbial fire. But the greater pleasure lies in the culmination of the growing season. It is the pleasure of acceptance, of letting be and letting go, of leaving things alone for awhile, until the time arrives to pitch in and clean up for another gardening year to come—or, more truly, for another gardening year that has already begun.

WHEN DOES AUTUMN begin? Fred Godomski, the meteorologist at Pennsylvania State University who prepares the daily weather maps for *The New York Times,* offers three different definitions. For astronomers, autumn is the season that begins with the fall equinox, when day and night are roughly equal in length, and ends three months later with the winter solstice, when the longest night of the year occurs. For meteorologists in North America, autumn begins on September 1 and ends on November 30. British and European meteorologists, however, reckon the season differently, as beginning August 1 and ending October 31. The precision of these definitions makes them useless for gardeners, since autumn in the garden begins at different times in different locations, and even in the same place gets underway on different days each year. I have one friend who says it starts when she notices the first small

The little pompons of a garden chrysanthemum intermingle with other plants and sprawl with casual charm to the pavement, as tall miscanthuses and pennisetums stand sentinel beyond.

leaves of chickweed. Another friend says that fall announces itself when he first detects the faint sweet smell of rotting leaves from some woods near his house.

My own definition, valid in most years in the spot I inhabit, places the onset of autumn sometime in mid-August. A day arrives that marks a turning, that whispers change. Rain falls that is slow and lingering. One night it is so cool that we are almost tempted to get out the featherbeds and stow the fans in the attic, although experience teaches that these acts would be folly: the dog days are not over just yet. In roadside ditches out in the country, the pearly, light pink buds of Joe Pye weed begin to open into fringed and fluffy flowers arranged in huge and commanding clusters that are beloved of swallowtail and monarch butterflies. In fields and in the wastelands behind grocery stores, the brassy hues of the earliest goldenrods are beginning to show, even as the white of Queen Anne's lace still spangles the earth. In the marshes near our house, pink and white wild mallows have started to bloom, sometimes with herons close by. In moist wooded areas along the highways, the tupelos show an occasional crimson leaf, a foretaste of the spectacle to come.

In the garden, the population of insects and spiders has changed its character, becoming a little more friendly to human beings—the biting flies and the mosquitos having vanished—if not more friendly among themselves. In the evening I watch a writing spider spin its web in the failing light. The net gets larger every twilight as the spider gorges itself on tinier prey. In the morning I find in the shrubbery the dew-covered webs of the spiders, which do scribble out something with their silk patterns that might be a signature, although none yet has thrilled me with the words SOME PIG. The last of the daylilies has finished blooming, and the first chore that feels like autumn will be to remove their unsightly brown scapes. *Clematis paniculata,* the sweet autumn clematis, spills over some large yews in a flood of thousands of little pure white flowers. Sedum 'Autumn Joy' has yet to bloom, but sedum 'Vera Jameson' has opened the first of its mauve-pink flower clusters, extremely handsome with its smoky purple leaves. The first boltonia flowers have appeared—just a few, but soon the plants will

The velvety blossoms of *Clematis viticella* 'Rubra' soften the harsh texture of a wall in mid-September, ending a season of bloom that started in July.

be covered. Aster 'Alma Potschke' is at its peak, and some of the later perennial asters show signs of buds. *Helianthus angustifolius* has now reached eight feet in height and started to branch out. It will not flower for two months yet, but the plant has become a looming presence. The garden now reminds me of a symphony orchestra tuning for a concert. Fall has not quite arrived in its full power and majesty, but the time will soon arrive for its long unfolding. It will end some time in early December, when the last flower of the 'Betty Prior' rose finally drops its petals and I think, once again, what a wonderful autumn it was.

Lingering Perennials

In some respects, gardening and music are kindred arts. They appeal to the senses, although music speaks primarily to hearing and gardening to vision, touch, hearing, smell, and even taste (as when a child breaks off honeysuckle blossoms and sips their nectar). They both unfold over time, in sequential order. They are arts of combination, and in each there are possibilities of both harmony and dissonance. They provide immediate emotional satisfactions to raw amateurs and novices, and yet they are so inexhaustible that neither gardener nor musician can ever reach the point of saying, "Ah, yes, now I know all that there is to know." Both are ruled by underlying scientific imperatives, although music is grounded primarily in physics, and gardening draws on a greater number of scientific disciplines, including chemistry, geology, biology, and astronomy.

But as I consider the sequence of the gardening year and its transition from summer into fall, a particular comparison with music suggests itself: the idea of pedal point. In classical music theory, pedal point is a sustained note, usually in the bass clef, which sounds over a long period, giving unity to the shifting harmonies of the other parts. The garden also has its pedal point, in the form of perennials which are of interest over a long period of time, either for their foliage or for a season of bloom that begins in late spring or early summer and continues well into fall. A garden may be transformed when the plants specific to autumn begin to bloom, but the lingerers, together with the architectural features of the garden such as pathways and walls and steps, give it a sense of unity over a longer period. And since these lingerers I speak of are perennials, they tie each year to the one which came before and to the one which will follow.

ACANTHUS

For the greater part of my life, until just recently in fact, all that I knew about *Acanthus mollis,* or bear's breeches, was that the Greeks thought so highly of its showy leaves that they used it as the motif adorning the capital of the Corinthian column, and I was nineteen before I possessed even that stray piece of information. Then my wife, Hella, returned one day from her annual pilgrimage to the Philadelphia Flower Show with the name of the same plant written down and the firm intention that we should lose no time in getting it into our garden. She said it was the most spectacular plant she had ever seen, with huge, bold, and glossy dark green leaves, a good many prickles, and spikes of lavender-mauve flowers that rose six feet high and looked down on an average beholder. I ordered a plant from a mail-order nursery I hadn't tried before. I don't to this day know what they sent and will never know, because a rabbit ate it, but Hella said it certainly wasn't the acanthus she wanted.

Then that summer, at the same nursery near Philadelphia that had forced it into early bloom for display at the flower show (acanthus ordinarily blooms in August, except in California, when its season is spring), I saw the real thing—spotted it from 150 feet away, in fact, for it was a mature specimen, roughly the size of a VW Beetle. It wasn't for sale, and a clerk told me that if it were, it would cost me at least $200. It wouldn't fit into the car trunk, anyway, so we paid $15 for a plant of more modest scale, brought it home, and put it in the kind of location it prefers—fairly shady, with moist soil rich in organic matter. It has steadily grown larger and more imposing, and promises to keep doing so for some time to come.

I am a little confused about the winter hardiness of acanthus. Some books say it's strictly a plant for Zone 8 and even milder zones; others claim that it will do fine in Zone 6 or even Zone 5. I can report only that it's fine in Zone 7, although I suspect the deep mulch of leaves we cover it with in late November is a needed safety net for especially severe winters. The foxglovelike flowers are handsome and dignified, and the August season of bloom almost qualifies it as a fall bloomer. But its lingering interest lies in the high drama of its imposingly large and very glossy leaves. Grown in shade, it will fail to flower but will still provide a focus of attention.

ARTEMISIAS

With the single exception of *Artemisia lactiflora,* which is grown for its huge and feathery plume of flowers in late summer and which has green leaves, the artemisias are primarily foliage plants, immensely valuable for their gray or silvery leaves. As more and more gray creeps into my hair, the same thing is happening in my garden. I even suspect that there's a rule here, that the longer people garden the more they appreciate plants with gray leaves. Gray, for one thing, is a great peacemaker among colors that otherwise would clash. Gray furthermore looks attractive even in the harsh light of a midsummer noon, when green goes flat and loses the richness it has in early morning or late afternoon. Plants with gray leaves are also tolerant of poor soil, and they can thrive

In late August the spiky plumes and soft, cool hue of *Artemisia lactiflora* contrast perfectly with the rich copper flowers of *Helenium* 'Moorheim Beauty' and the prickly globes of *Echinops ritro*.

on low rations of moisture, no mean advantage in time of drought. Their only requirement is full sun.

One artemisia, *A. schmidtiana* 'Silver Mound', is possibly the single most widely grown perennial in the nursery trade. Our large wholesale nurseries propagate it by the millions, and there is scarcely a garden center in the country that doesn't sell great numbers of 'Silver Mound' in containers every spring. Its color is indeed the closest thing to true silver in a plant that I have seen, and it has much charm and elegance. It also has a couple of flaws that have earned it some instructive nicknames. Its strong propensity to collapse in hot and humid weather makes the wary call it "Silver Heap." Its frequent failure to survive the winter causes some people to call it "Nurseryman's Friend."

'Silver Mound', however, is the only temperamental and chancy artemisia I know. The genus is filled with thugs. 'Silver King' and 'Silver Queen' are both highly praised, but they gallop and romp, especially if they are planted in rich, moist soil. Some people plant them in large pots sunk in the ground, so they can lift them from time to time to make certain that their vigorous stolons don't escape and spread everywhere. I planted these two artemisias several years ago, and wish I'd followed this good counsel. But I put up with the constant need to rip them out where they are unwelcome, because their soothing gray color more than makes up for their pushy ways. And these three are perfect gentry, as compared to *A. purshiana.* This gangster came as a bonus a few years ago with an order of plants from a mail-order nursery, and I wish I'd looked this particular gift horse in the mouth. It spread twelve feet in one summer, and that was just for starters. I will probably never eradicate it.

Fortunately, there are artemisias that are not bent on conquering the world. 'Valerie Finnis', which has very downy silver-gray leaves and grows to two feet or so, stays in place with unusual restraint for an artemisia. 'Powis Castle', which is fairly woody, with round clusters of finely cut blue-gray foliage, also behaves itself. It combines excellently with blue Lyme grass *(Elymus canadensis)*, which insinuates itself and its graceful, arching leaves up through the similarly colored but contrasting textures of this arte-

The silvery-gray artemisias make a fine foil for flowers of more intense colors. At left, *Artemisia* 'Powis Castle' swirls around *Viola* 'Arkwright Ruby', an indefatigable bloomer from early summer to late autumn. At right, the seed plumes of *A.* 'Valerie Finnis' set off the dark beauty of *Aster* 'Hella Lacy'.

misia. These two plants can carry a corner of a garden all by themselves from spring to fall, but a splendid added touch of spice comes if the glowing orange crocosmia 'Emily McKenzie' joins the ensemble. Its swordlike leaves lend a contrasting texture to the other foliage, and the arrogant color of its flowers is tamed by the blue-grays nearby.

The artemisia closest to my heart is *A. versicolor*. This one is lean, gaunt, and rather skeletal. In its gray sparseness, it works very well next to the silken opulence of heuchera 'Palace Purple', with its large, slightly crinkled leaves of brownish purple. It is also good with another long bloomer, *Malva alcea* 'Fastigiata', which keeps producing little hollyhocklike blossoms deep into September—but then, almost any gray artemisia consorts nicely with almost any other plant.

Some of the artemisias bring with them some fascinating lore and history, real or imagined. *Artemisia vulgaris,* or mugwort, a weed no one would plant deliberately, was thought by medieval herbalists to keep away both lightning and unwanted visitors if hung in a doorway. *A. absinthium,* which, legend has it, arose from the tracks of the serpent in Eden right after it tempted our first parents, was an essential ingredient in absinthe, the liquor that rotted the brains of so many nineteenth-century Parisian artists and bohemians. And *A. abrotanum,* variously known as southernwood, lad's love, and maiden's ruin, was at one time thought to be a sure cure for baldness if mixed with oil and rubbed on the scalp.

ASTEROMOEA MONGOLICA

I will call this charming plant by this name because it is so listed in the catalogues of several nurseries, although the name is in doubt. Some think it is really *Boltonia indica,* although *Kalimeris pinnifitida* is also possible. In the South, it goes from one gardener to another under the name Oxford orphanage plant, because it once grew in abundance on the grounds of the orphanage in Oxford, North Carolina. Whatever its botanical name may be, it is a prime example of the role only one person may play in keeping a plant going that otherwise might be lost. In *A Southern*

Garden (1942), Elizabeth Lawrence tells the story of getting *A. mongolica* from a friend in Greensboro who had in her turn gotten it from a nursery that had since gone out of business. Miss Lawrence was so fond of it that she distributed it widely among her own friends, who after her death in 1985 saw to it that Holbrook Farm and Nursery, Montrose Nursery, and We-Du Nurseries received stock to propagate for their customers.

Whatever its name, anyone who grows it owes a debt to Elizabeth Lawrence, for it's an excellent and trouble-free long-blooming perennial. It grows about two feet tall, with a very dainty and delicate form, quite open and airy. The multitude of little pompom flowers from midsummer until the first killing freeze look like a doll's powderpuffs—or like tiny double Shasta daisies, white, with a buttery yellow center. When the nights turn cool, it takes on a faint cast of pale lilac. It is winter hardy to Zone 6 at least. It spreads by underground roots, but not aggressively enough to worry the faint of heart.

COREOPSIS

One of the casualties of real-estate development in my county is a field that has now become a supermarket parking lot. The soil was poor there, and before the land was bulldozed and the asphalt went down, it stayed bright all summer with the kinds of wildflowers that thrive on well-drained soil of low fertility. In July and August there were great masses of butterfly weed or *Asclepias tuberosa,* but the grandest show of the year always came in late May and early June, when the entire field was a solid golden sheet of *Coreopsis grandiflora,* a southern and southwestern species which escaped from northeastern gardens to fields and roadsides sometime in the nineteenth century, assuming the life of an amiable tramp. I miss the sight of this particular coreopsis, but nevertheless would not want to bring it back to a more domesticated life in my own garden. Even in lean soil, it is a flopsy thing, and in richer and moister soil it falls over under the weight of its own blossoms, looking as if some terrible freak windstorm had just passed through.

Fortunately there are other coreopsis which behave themselves with perfect comportment in the garden. Two of them, 'Sunray' and 'Goldfink', are highly refined cultivars of *Coreopsis grandiflora*. 'Sunray' is restrained in its habit, growing only to eighteen inches with a somewhat mounded form. It blooms freely and generously, bearing great numbers of double golden flowers from early summer right through September. 'Goldfink', whose name (referring to a finch, not a fink) proclaims that it is one of those native American perennials that have been transformed by the work of German hybridizers, is a dwarf, growing under ten inches high and bearing rich yellow blossoms over a very long season.

Among other coreopsis, three cultivars of our native thread-leafed coreopsis, *Coreopsis verticillata,* are attractive both for their delicate foliage and their prolific bloom. 'Golden Shower'—well, the name says it all. It grows to about two feet high, as does a suitable companion called 'Moonbeam', which bears a great many

Aster frikartii 'Mönch' and *Co-reopsis* 'Zagreb' make excellent companions over a prolonged season of bloom. Here, they are in their prime in early September in a garden in Portland, Oregon.

pale cream to primrose yellow blossoms over a long season. ('Moon-beam', it should be noted, may be short lived in many gardens, especially after a harsh winter with no protective snow cover. I have sometimes lost it, and I waste no time in replacing it, as it's high on my list of indispensable perennials.) The third cultivar is 'Za-greb', with deep yellow flowers on compact plants that seldom exceed twelve inches. These three derivatives of the native thread-leafed coreopsis are very useful in front of daylilies, since their feathery texture lightens the heavy, clunky look of daylily leaves.

Another worthy coreopsis is *Coreopsis auriculata* 'Nana', a rock-garden plant that grows only ten inches high. This dwarf variety, with large, fragrant, coppery-orange single flowers whose petals have appealing notched edges, is also called the Maysville daisy, after the town in Kentucky near the limestone cliffs where a botanist, Lucy Braun, discovered it in the 1920s. It is generally considered to be a May and June bloomer, but I have seen it in sporadic bloom well into November and heard reports of a stray blossom on Christmas day. It combines well with another native perennial wildflower, *Chrysogonum virginianum,* whose common names include green-and-gold, golden star, and pots of gold. This chrysogonum seldom aspires beyond five inches in height, and its single composite flowers echo the form of *Coreopsis auriculata* 'Nana', but in a softer shade of gold. It blooms persistently, almost relentlessly, from April onward. Unlike coreopsis, which relishes a fully sunny location, green-and-gold grows well in partial shade. The two plants may thus be massed together where full sun and light shade meet, so that the chrysogonums will carry the gleam of gold back into the dimmer light, bringing warmth and brightness.

Coreopsis are so strongly associated with shades of yellow and gold that *Coreopsis rosea* comes as a surprise. As the species name indicates, it bears soft pink flowers. They are tiny, about half the size of a dime. Bloom is nonstop from summer into fall. It grows only twelve inches high, and its spreading, stoloniferous habit makes it a good ground cover for either full sun or light shade. The narrow leaves, a crisp green in summer, turn a glowing shade of golden tan in the fall. The only source I know for this seldom-grown but promising northeastern perennial is Canyon Creek Nursery,

The contrasting textures of the foliage of *Coreopsis* 'Moonbeam' and *Verbena tenuisecta* would be appealing even if the flowers did not harmonize together so splen-didly.

although some wholesale nurseries are beginning to take an interest in propagating it on a large scale. I hear rumors of a white form. I also harbor the suspicion, based on the stoloniferous habit of *C. rosea* and its equal success in sun or shade (plus a few rumblings from friends with whom I exchange tales of greedy plants that exceed in their takeover ambitions anything seen on Wall Street), that this coreopsis needs to be watched closely and vetted if it starts wanting *Lebensraum.* (The fears of "creeping Communism" with which we alarmed ourselves for some decades after World War II because of galloping Nazism, and our rhetoric about eternal vigilance, may finally prove unfounded. But any garden is liable to harbor creeping Communists, Trojan Horses, or what you will.)

THE CHOCOLATE COSMOS

Like Maria in *The Sound of Music,* I have my list of favorite things. It includes both cosmos and chocolate, so it's no surprise that as soon as I heard that there was a cosmos that smelled like chocolate, I ordered three plants right away. It is *Cosmos atrosanguineus,* a half-hardy perennial. It does indeed have a rich bitter-chocolate scent that intensifies in the afternoon. The single flowers, almost three inches across, are dark cordovan maroon verging on black, with a velvety look and feel. The plants have an airy habit and some tendency to lean, a trait that can be turned to advantage by allowing their stems and opulent blossoms to weep down toward some other plants with pleasingly contrasting or complementary colors. A half-dozen white annual alyssums planted in front of or intermingled with just three chocolate cosmos make a fine contrast. The combination seems to bring a new freshness to the white of the alyssums and to deepen the color of the cosmos blossoms to a rich shade of black cherry. If 'Rose Queen' alyssums are substituted, instead of a contrast there's a quiet harmony, something like a duet between two contraltos. But whether you strive for visual contrast or for harmony, the combination of fragrances will be equally delicious, as the light honey scent of alyssum mingles with the deeper chocolate fragrance of this cosmos.

The only bad news about *Cosmos atrosanguineus* is that it is

An eye-pleasing combination results when *Artemisia* 'Silver Queen' and *Geranium* 'Ann Folkard' sing in harmony with the chocolate cosmos *(C. atrosanguineus)*. Who could resist a flower with such a rich, velvety color that also smells of chocolate?

reliably winter hardy only to Zone 9. It forms tubers, somewhat like those of dahlias but harder to store over the winter without their shriveling to nothing. The trick is to put these plants into the garden in one-gallon plastic pots which you sink in the ground, and then bring pot and all inside to dry out after the first killing freeze. The insulation provided by the soil will keep the tubers plump and sound. The pots should be brought to a cool, bright place such as a sun porch in late winter and watered well to initiate growth about six weeks before planting time in late May. The tubers may be divided, but the likely result will be spotty bloom, as the chocolate cosmos is somewhat finicky to establish. A better way of increasing the plants is to take cuttings of the first new growth, which root easily.

Again, the only source I know for *Cosmos atrosanguineus* is Canyon Creek Nursery. And—I swear it—I don't own stock in the company.

DIANTHUS

The affections of gardeners for the perennial dianthuses, or pinks, are as ancient and passionate as they are for roses, lavenders, and lilacs—other plants that also have lent their names to colors. Many, if not all, are fragrant and spicy. They bloom generously in late spring and early summer, and then their season is over, except for the occasional sporadic flower, which is always welcome when it appears. But their mats or low mounds of closely placed foliage lend interest even when no blossom is in sight and form an effective barrier against many weeds.

I find the dianthuses with gray or blue-gray leaves, which often persist all through the winter in my own garden, to be uncommonly soothing to the eye. 'Aqua' has quite bluish foliage and large, double, white flowers that are intensely fragrant. 'Gold Dust' makes a cushion of gray, and its large, dark red blossoms are spotted with flecks of gold and the petals fringed on their edges. 'Helen,' with semidouble salmon flowers, forms a good cushion of gray leaves and blooms over a much longer season than other perennial dianthuses, right into October. Among the species with gray foliage,

Dianthus alpinus, D. simulans, and *D. subacaulis* are all worth-while. Dianthuses are easy, provided that they are given well-drained and gritty soil. They may be mulched with a thin layer of small stones, but never with organic matter. One summer I treated a collection of some twenty different kinds to a mulch of shredded bark two inches deep, thinking I was helping them cope with a bad drought. I had no idea what I was doing. Half the plants rotted the following winter from too much moisture around their crowns, and the rest looked iffy until I moved them to another, unmulched spot.

DICENTRA

When the eastern American native plant *Dicentra eximia,* commonly known as squirrel corn, begins blooming in late April or early May, wildflower lovers can get a little giddy. Frances Theodora Parsons, in *According to Season* (1902), thought this plant the "crowning glory" of the woodland, praising the "great soft masses of the finely cut leaves of the squirrel corn, with here and there a spike of pale-pink, heart-shaped flowers." At that time of the year, however, my affections lie with another dicentra altogether, the Japanese species *Dicentra spectabilis,* the old-fashioned bleeding heart, with its graceful, arching sprays of long stems bearing lockets of flowers, either soft pink or pure white, depending on the kind. By autumn, however, my mind has always changed. The bleeding heart blooms only briefly, and it lapses into dormancy after a long and unsightly period of yellowing agony. *Dicentra eximia,* in contrast, flowers over a long period that stretches well into October, with the heaviest bloom in the spring but with suffi-cient flowers later in the season to make it well worth growing. It is a fine plant for moist semishade (a bit deeper shade in Zone 8 and warmer areas). The delicate blue-green foliage forms a mound about ten inches high. The flowers, smaller and looser versions of the lockets of its bleeding heart kin, are borne outward and upward from the clump. A western species, *D. formosa,* is quite similar if a bit shorter. Its steel-blue foliage changes in the autumn to an arresting shade of pumpkin. Several hybrid cultivars between these two species flower more freely than their parents. 'Snowdrift' (no huge surprise here) is white, 'Luxuriant' cherry-rose, and 'Zestful' strong, clear pink. All will tolerate sizzling summer heat as well as winter temperatures below −20 degrees. The woodland habitat of the species indicates their appreciation of soil rich in humus, but these derivatives of *Dicentra eximia* are remarkably forgiving of inconsiderate treatment.

Apart from their cheerful flowers, these dicentras have such highly attractive foliage as to invite experiments in plant combination. I place them near other plants of similar delicacy, such as dwarf astilbes like *Astilbe chinensis* 'Pumila' and especially 'Sprite', which has wonderful bronze-red foliage. Other plants with bolder foliage, such as bergenias, also work well with dicentras, and their persistent evergreen winter foliage lends additional interest when the dicentras are dormant. Bergenia 'Sunningdale' is an especially choice cultivar for its wine-red rosettes of leaves after the temperature plunges.

ERYSIMUM 'BOWLES MAUVE'

This perennial wallflower is the indisputable champion as far as length of blooming season is concerned. When I first got it as a small rooted cutting late one October, it was already blooming at just three inches high, with sweetly fragrant, light purple flowers. It was still blooming at Christmas, and it came into flower again during a mild spell in mid-January. Heavy and nonstop bloom begins in March. The long and narrow bluish-green leaves remain throughout the winter. This super erysimum, which produces no seed and must be propagated vegetatively, forms a shrubby mound some eighteen inches tall and wide. It is winter hardy at least to Zone 7, although it tends to be short lived, so that cuttings should be started in late summer and overwintered in a cold frame as a safeguard to keep it going.

FERNS

Any garden with some shade in it stands incomplete, I think, unless it has at least a few ferns. And I know some handsome gardens where they dominate almost to the exclusion of other herbaceous plants. Now in her eighties, my friend Hannah Withers simplified her walled garden in Charlotte, North Carolina, a few years ago. Besides a sunny little patch of lawn that she hires someone to mow every week and pots of geraniums and small-flowered roses on her patio, she grows a limited but choice repertoire of plants, each in huge masses or drifts. Her brick walls are covered with the very handsome evergreen clematis, *Clematis armandii* (not winter hardy, alas, north of Zone 8). She has several colonies of *Arum italicum* 'Pictum'. This plant, which in England goes by the common name of lords-and-ladies, is fetching in late spring for flowers much resembling those of jack-in-the-pulpit, bold and handsome in late summer for its large spikes of glowing red fruits, and lovely in the fall for its new growth of fresh green leaves stippled and marbled with creamy white. Hannah has hellebores, hundreds and hundreds of them, self-sown over many years. But most of all, Hannah has ferns, thousands of plants representing virtually every genus and species with ornamental value that will grow in her part of the South.

I claim nothing similar, but my garden gets fernier every year. I like the very idea of ferns. They provide a sense of connection that goes pretty far back, to indulge in understatement. The first ferns appeared on earth around 380 million years ago, beating the first reptiles by 70 million years. North America and Europe were still joined in one continent. The very antiquity of the ferns would be good reason for growing at least a few, just for old times' sake. But there are aesthetic reasons, too. It's hard even to think about ferns without words like "graceful" and "elegant" springing to mind. They bring to gardens a woodsy feeling, a hint of wildness and coolness.

None of my ferns is especially rare, but they all have uncommon beauty. The maidenhair fern, *Adiantum pedatum*, which is winter hardy to Zone 2, is hard to beat for its glossy and wiry black stems and its fronds with leaflets (are they frondlets?) that spread out in a horseshoe shape. In the slightest breeze, the fronds tremble and flutter as if they were about to take flight. As for *Athyrium filix-femina*, or lady fern, it is even hardier, to Zone 1, and under wet conditions its fronds easily reach three feet. It is deciduous, and especially lovely in autumn, when it turns copper and apricot and soft gold. The latest things in ferns, by which I mean only the latest ferns that a lot of gardeners have pounced on, are in the same genus. These are the Japanese painted ferns. Easiest to come by, although it's not exactly as plentiful as impatiens, is *A. goeringianum* 'Pictum', sometimes listed as *A. nipponicum* 'Pictum'. I know of no foliage plant that surpasses it in subtle beauty of color. The deeply cut and divided fronds crowd together thickly in clumps about fifteen inches high. The stems and veins are a deep old-rose or crushed mulberry. The color suffuses into the center of each leaflet. Toward the outer edge there is first a band of silver gray and then another of pale olive. Here grace and elegance sing in harmony. There is at least one variant form sold under the same name that has strong reddish overtones. A closely related species, *A. iseanum* 'Pictum', is pewter and raspberry-mauve. It grows only to eight inches and thus is splendid planted in front of its taller kin, looking something like a little wave swirling ahead of a larger one. Any of the painted ferns looks terrific combined with almost any other plants. I grow them near heuchera 'Palace Purple' and some hardy pink oxalis of unknown identity, and something about the combination of textures and smoky colors makes me feel content.

Not very far away, other ferns that like wet feet are planted in our bog, which lies in shade half the day except in winter. They are associated with a fine iris called 'Aichi', which came to me years ago identified as a yellow Japanese iris, although it's a hybrid between *Iris ensata* (the real "Japanese iris," formerly *I. kaempferi*) and the European species, *I. pseudacorus.* The flowers are indeed yellow, but the best thing about this plant is that its leaves are yellow too, a fine translucent yellow that captures the sunlight until the plant seems to glow from within. This yellow is wonderful with the frank greens of the ferns nearby. One is *Dryopteris marginalis,* the marginal wood fern, which grows two feet and stays green throughout autumn and winter. Two others are osmundas. *Osmunda cinnamomea,* the cinnamon fern, grows to four feet, while *O. regalis,* the royal fern, tops out a foot higher with its tiers of horizontal fronds. In the same spot, there's a fine specimen of

Matteuccia struthiopteris or ostrich fern, which also attains five feet. The interplay of these ferns, similar but also different, like variations on a theme, is deeply satisfying, and they all work well with some of the late-flowering perennials that are their bogmates, including *Lobelia cardinalis* and *L. siphilitica.* In late autumn, the deciduous ferns, now pale yellow or bronze depending on the kind, go into a semicollapse, like Mimi near the end of *La Bohème,* bringing a fine sense of the near completion of another year.

A last curiosity, though not reliably winter hardy above Zone 8, is the Japanese climbing fern, *Lygodium japonicum,* which I keep in a pot and bring inside for the winter. Even where it is hardy, it is deciduous, dying back to the ground completely once the temperature drops below freezing. But it emerges early in the spring and grows rapidly to a height of seven feet, supporting itself by weaving through other vegetation or up a fence or trellis. One of its best uses is along a chain-link fence, whose ugly dog-kennel look it softens with a mist of green.

HARDY FUCHSIAS

There comes a point in the lives of most gardeners when they perk up their ears on hearing the word "hardy." Fairly early in our horticultural self-education, we learn to sort things into tidy categories. This plant is a perennial, that one an annual, and the one over yonder a biennial. Or this one is hardy and that one too tender to survive much winter to speak of. But we snap to attention when we hear described as hardy a plant we have previously ticketed as tender. Hardy begonias *(Begonia grandis)* are one example. The several species of fall- and winter-blooming hardy cyclamens are another. And a third example are the hardy fuchsias, whose very existence can come as a great surprise.

I saw my first hardy fuchsias in England in 1970. They were growing in the cloister of Chester Cathedral—substantial bushes five feet high and seven feet across, loaded down with hundreds of tiny, graceful pendant blossoms of ruby and amethyst and with equal numbers of glossy, blackish-red seed capsules. In the golden light of a English afternoon in late August, these shrubs were afire

Although it dies back to the ground where winters are fierce, *Fuchsia magellanica* is a magnificent small shrub in milder regions, as here, lining a watercourse in the VanDuzen Botanical Garden in Vancouver, British Columbia.

with glory. Their blossoms obviously identified them as fuchsias, but they were far tinier than the tender fuchsias I knew. A gardener working in the cloister identified them as *Fuchsia magellanica.* When she added that they were hardy, I took her word for it but filed the information away with two words added: "in England." Later I read about hedges of fuchsias in Cornwall and in Ireland. Hardy ones "in Cornwall." "In Ireland." The way plants behave in Great Britain and in Ireland is no sure-fire guide to their performance in most of the United States, except sometimes (not always) in the Pacific Northwest.

Hardy fuchsias, *F. magellanica* and its several cultivars, do in fact grow in the Pacific Northwest as they do in Great Britain. In both places, they are woody plants, shrubs which suffer little dieback in the winter. They bloom profusely over a long season from early summer to late fall, bearing heavy crops of fruits that make a passable jam. I decided to take a chance with these fuchsias one spring when I found eight different cultivars in the catalogue of Lamb Nursery, in Spokane. The catalogue said give them a shady location, so I did, with one exception. I thought it might be nice to have a fuchsia out by the mailbox, so I planted one called 'Señorita' there, even though it was in full sun. It was a small plant, but it quickly grew into an upright shrub about three feet high. By August it was in such generous bloom, rich little red and purple flowers, that it evoked memories of the Chester cloister. The abundant bloom went on until the first hard freeze. It was quite a show from a $2 plant, and I decided that if it died over the winter—and I was sure it would—I would simply replace it the next year and in years to come.

The other seven fuchsias, the ones placed in shade, just sulked, bloomed unenthusiastically, and didn't come back the next spring. 'Señorita' died back to the roots, and it took its own sweet time in making a reappearance, but in the middle of May fresh new shoots sprang up around the previous year's woody stems. That was in 1975. 'Señorita' has come back every year since, so I feel confident about its winter hardiness in Zone 7. Since then, I've added other appealing cultivars. 'Tom Thumb' grows only about a foot high and bears tiny flowers quite similar in color to those of 'Señorita'. 'Maiden's Blush' reaches almost to four feet, has light green leaves, and produces lavish numbers of little pale pink blossoms. 'Bashful' is a dwarf plant, only fourteen inches tall, with double white flowers veined red. It has received an Award of Merit from the Royal Horticultural Society. 'Wicked Queen'—do this name and that of 'Bashful' reflect the influence of Walt Disney?—has dark red sepals and double deep purple petals splashed with pink and white. Some other hardy fuchsias contribute interesting foliage as well as flowers. 'Gracilis' has dark green leaves veined crimson to match the color of its blossoms. 'Aurea' has bright chartreuse leaves and

Fuchsia 'Gartenmeister Bonnstedt' looks like clusters of Chinese firecrackers ready to explode.

crimson flowers. The flowers of 'Versicolor' are a rich red, the leaves a smoky combination of cream and gray and rose. All are fine lingerers, adding grace notes, and many of them, to the autumn garden.

Despite their winter hardiness thus far, I must add that there are always some jittery moments before these hardy fuchsias return, and in fact some care is needed to help them survive. Last year's growth shouldn't be removed until the new growth shows. The old wood protects the plant, as does a deep mulch. Fertilizer is best avoided until warm weather spurs vegetative growth. One caveat is in order for people who garden where the night temperatures can drop into the mid-20s as late as the beginning of May. New plants ordered in the spring from nurseries on the West Coast, the best sources for fuchsias, are likely to be so soft and tender that a sudden late freeze may kill them, roots and all. Wisdom calls for planting them temporarily in pots that may be kept inside in a cool and sunny place before they go into a more permanent location in the garden.

Exactly how hardy are hardy fuchsias? A quick check of the reference books shows some disagreement, with estimates ranging from Zone 7 to Zone 5. I know someone in the icebox of Connecticut, in its northwestern corner and closer to Zone 4 than 5, who grows some unidentified cultivar of *F. magellanica.* She always mulches it. Just to be on the safe side, she roots cuttings in late summer and brings them inside. Some years the plant in her garden comes through the winter splendidly. Some years she loses it. She has a true gardener's spirit: she takes risks and chances, but she also takes precautions.

GAILLARDIA

Among the cultivars of perennial gaillardia currently in the nursery trade, a few commend themselves especially for the summer garden, because of their clear, unmixed colors. These include 'Burgundy' (large wine-red daisies), 'The Sun' (golden-yellow ones), and some others. But it seems to be in the very nature of the gaillardia to dress itself in colors few people would deliberately put together, particularly under a blazing hot sun. These colors are red and yellow—the strongly red centers of the ray flowers edged with equally strong yellow. They are difficult to combine in the same perennial border, unless they are sharply segregated from one another by a great deal of gray foliage to keep the peace. When they combine in the same flower, the result may be a vision of paradise for honeybees, but it's a field of battle for human onlookers. Louise Beebe Wilder made the definitive statement in *Colour in My Garden* (1918): "Yellow and red is of all colour combinations to me the most unpleasant. . . . Gaillardias I particularly dislike, save the pure yellow Lady Rolleston." But she relented in her opposition to the usual gaillardias once autumn arrived: "Yet I always admire them warmly when I see them in my friends' autumn gardens. . . . Purple, scarlet, and gold," she wrote, "are the colours of the autumn garden, and however bizarre and extravagant their assemblage, the eye is made quiet, not only by means of its harmony with the season, but through its accordance with the moods of our own mind."

There may be in Mrs. Wilder's remarks about the sudden acceptability red-and-yellow gaillardias take on in autumn a hint for an imaginative hybridizer to begin the quest for a strain that would sit out the summer, waiting until the decent cool of mid-September to start strutting itself. Meanwhile, gaillardias are proficient lingerers, plants of summer that continue into the fall, when their hot and warring colors lose their touch of alarm and actually warm the spirit. Some worthy ones are 'Baby Cole,' a dwarf cultivar that grows only eight inches high, and the taller strains 'Goblin' and 'Torchlight'.

GAURA

I have said so much in favor of *Gaura lindheimeri*, a tall perennial native to Texas, that friends have accused me of wanting to start the American Gaura Society. So I'll begin here with the plant's shortcomings. It seems to perform best in a light and sandy soil, exactly what I've got. Allen Bush, whose soil in North Carolina tends more toward clay, says that he finds gaura can vary considera-

The gaudy pinwheels of gaillardia contribute great warmth and good cheer in the late-season garden. Here is *Gaillardia x grandiflora* 'Bremen'.

bly in performance from one year to the next. Gaura also may be a short-lived perennial where the winters are really cold, but it self-seeds freely and blooms in under three months after germination. It looks a bit ratty by the end of autumn—Hella says by the end of June—but if it's cut back sharply in midsummer, it stays tidy looking, though still tall at about four feet. And the irregular magenta blotches that appear on the foliage remind me of blood blisters, not exactly a great aesthetic plus.

I have no plans to found the A.G.S., but I'm still keen on gaura. It is highly drought-resistant, no slight virtue in a time when "xeriscaping" is become so familiar a term that it's hardly necessary to explain that it means gardening practices that conserve water. The blossoms, like little white butterflies, are borne on willowy, graceful stems that constantly elongate. Gaura is a fine plant to use as a "scrim." The term is borrowed from the theater, where it means a gauze curtain through which action on stage may be seen, but as if through a mist. A scrim plant is a tall one which may be placed at the front of a flower border, where it partially, but not totally, conceals the plants behind or beyond it. My own little colony of gauras grows in wood chips in front of a flower border, not in the border itself. (This trick is useful with other plants as well, if it's not overdone. It blurs the usual lines of distinction, and it makes certain plants like gauras into solo performers instead of members of an ensemble.)

Gauras keep blooming almost to early November. By then they flower sparsely, but the stems have turned a deep maroon-red that itself is interesting as they sway in the wind. The color of the stems gradually fades to a soft tan. If they are left standing over winter, the plants do something quite remarkable, something I've noticed in no other perennials. They twist inward on themselves in a spiral or corkscrew motion, looking by midwinter as forlorn and lovely as driftwood on a desolate beach.

HOSTAS

Hostas do bloom, producing spikes of bell-like flowers that may be white or blue purple and that may appear any time from early

Three bold emblems of the fall garden: the ornamental grass *Miscanthus sinensis* 'Gracillimus' at its peak of bloom, *Sedum* 'Autumn Joy' living up to its name, and *Hosta sieboldiana*, its grand leaves starting to turn. The leaves of many hostas take on a new and warmer beauty as they begin to melt and crinkle and turn color after early frosts.

summer to late September depending on the kind, but the flowers have so small a part in the appeal of hostas that some people remove the spikes when they first show. Hostas are foliage plants par excellence, and they are very diverse in their characteristics. Some are so tiny that they may disappear overnight, since slugs are even fonder of hostas than members of the American Hosta Society are, if such a thing be possible. Others, such as *Hosta sieboldiana* 'Elegans', grow taller and wider than a washtub. The foliage may be green, or it may be tinged with blue or be a radiant gold. Many hostas combine several colors, with fascinating marbling, streaking, and splashing of white, gold, gray-blue, chartreuse, gold, and green in striking patterns. The leaves may be lance shaped, heart shaped, cupped, or even puckered like seersucker.

I've never seen a hosta I didn't like, but I do have some favorites. I'm especially partial to those with golden leaves, which pump color into dull and shady corners. 'Sum and Substance', which has slightly pleated leaves somewhere between chartreuse and pale gold, grows to true immensity after several seasons. Its cupped foliage rises three feet tall at the center of the plant and spans four feet. Just one plant is as emphatic as a manifesto. Only slightly smaller, at about 2½ feet high and 3 feet wide, 'Piedmont Gold' also offers a dramatic accent. Still smaller, 'Golden Tiara' is a little gumdrop of a plant, only a foot high. Among the blues (which by midsummer lose the waxy coating that gives them most of their color), I have considerable affection for 'Blue Umbrellas', 'Hadspen Blue', and 'Halcyon'. I also like 'Antioch' and 'Louisa', both bearing green leaves bordered in white. The best known hosta of them all, 'Frances Williams', has very large, slightly cupped leaves mingling blue-green with splashes of gold from their edges, in a highly intricate pattern.

The hosta season ends with the first good freeze, but some cultivars, such as *H. sieboldiana* 'Elegans', give a fine display of color as they collapse and die back. They have a melancholy look, like proud warriors badly beaten by an enemy, but their tones of burnt umber, peachy gold, and apricot are radiant in morning light as they decline.

LAMIUM AND LAMIASTRUM

Lamium used to be only a name in the ground cover section of nursery catalogues, in the pages I generally skip over in the belief that covering the ground, and the plants that do so, are among the lesser thrills of a gardener's life. Then a friend gave me two small plants of lamium 'Beacon Silver' and 'White Nancy'. Both have agreeably silver-spattered leaves. Both spread quickly, but not uncontrollably. (This last claim I might one of these days have to take back: gardeners are the ultimate revisionists; our firmest certainties about a plant's unalloyed merits have ways of changing to the realization that we have made a bad misjudgment.) 'Beacon Silver' bears deep old-rose flowers in clusters, 'White Nancy', white ones. Another wonderful lamium is 'Aureum', which has bright chartreuse leaves that keep their color all year. These three lamiums bloom constantly from late spring until very late autumn. They don't seem to know the meaning of a killing freeze. They will never attract the affection that has been lavished on the rose, the dahlia, or even (here and there), the gaura. But they are steady and reliable and giving, and their handsome foliage persists into winter, its silvery gleam a nice match in the morning for the crystals of frost that form on their leaves.

These three lamiums are fairly well behaved, but they will swamp perennials of lower height, such as violets. They are fine, however, as a carpet below more assertive plants. 'Beacon Silver' makes a nice combination swirling around the extremely hardy and hearty chrysanthemum 'Mei-Kyo'. The strange raspberry-sherbet color of the tiny button blossoms of 'Mei-Kyo' can be discordant, but it is fairly well tamed by the silvery foliage of this lamium and by the soft mauve overtones of its particular shade of pink.

Closely related to lamium is lamiastrum. *Lamiastrum galeobdolon* 'Variegatum' blooms only in late spring, with highly attractive spikes of butter-yellow flowers, but this somewhat aggressive ground cover remains attractive year round for its silver-splashed leaves. The cultivar 'Herman's Pride' is neater and more tailored in its silver variegation, and it remains in a clump.

The tall spikes of *Lobelia splendens* rise above a spreading tide of gloriosa daisies in this garden in British Columbia.

RUDBECKIAS

If I were starting a garden from scratch in a sunny spot, wanted bright color quickly, needed a steady source of excellent cut flowers, and had no budget to speak of, there's no question about what I would plant—the hybrid rudbeckias called gloriosa daisies. These short-lived perennials are aptly named indeed, for they are one of the glories of the garden from summer into fall.

Their care is simple. They germinate quickly from seed sown either in early spring or fall. Once established, they are reliable self-sowers, without making pests of themselves. They can stand

hot, dry weather that leaves many other flowers limp and miserable.

Gloriosa daisies, moreover, are so diverse in color and form that they might almost make a garden all by themselves. No two plants are exactly alike. Heights range from fifteen to thirty inches. The blossoms vary in size from two to six inches across. Most are single, but some are double or semidouble. The dominant color of the petals or ray flowers is deep gold, with a brown cone at the center, but there are also shades of russet and mahogany and copper, as well as some appealing combinations of the basic colors. In some strains, the cones are green.

When I consider the dazzling effect of a mass of gloriosas, as bright in the garden as the brass section in a symphony orchestra, I might wonder why Vincent van Gogh didn't do for them what he did for sunflowers—but the answer is easy. He couldn't paint gloriosa daisies because there weren't any in his day. They are in fact almost newcomers on the gardening scene. Introduced in the mid-1950s, they are younger than many a gardener who grows them.

Seed catalogues seldom contain any history of the seeds they offer, and that's a pity. Every plant has its story, and knowing it gives gardening an extra dimension of pleasure. The story of the gloriosa somewhat resembles the tale of Eliza Doolittle and her transformation by Professor Henry Higgins, except that here the professor's name was Blakeslee.

Gloriosas owe their toughness and their radiant summer color to their ancestor, one of the quintessentially American wildflowers of roadsides and open fields, the black-eyed Susan *(Rudbeckia hirta)*. Native to the midwestern states, this rudbeckia hitchhiked its way to the eastern seaboard in shipments of hay and clover in the nineteenth century, quickly making itself at home. Even in its natural state, the black-eyed Susan is worthy of a place in the garden, but it had a more glamorous future in store for it than wildflower-lovers could imagine, thanks to Professor Alfred Francis Blakeslee (1874–1954), director of the Genetics Experiment Station at Smith College, in Northampton, Massachusetts. In the later years of his life, Professor Blakeslee took the humble black-eyed Susan in hand. Treating the seeds with the chemical colchicine, he

Gloriosa daisies (foreground) and Michaelmas daisies, like 'Winston Churchill', are both native North American wildflowers that hybridizers have treated to a college education.

produced tetraploid black-eyed Susans—plants with double the usual number of chromosomes. The extra chromosomes brought greater vigor and enlarged possibilities for selective breeding to produce new colors and forms.

David Burpee eventually acquired stock of these tetraploid black-eyed Susans and instructed his seed company's breeders in California to improve them even further. Some forty acres were given over to these plants. Superior ones were tagged for keeping, the rest rogued out and discarded. Burpee's goals were large flowers on compact plants, wide variations in color, and boldness of effect.

Mr. Burpee introduced his gloriosas in 1957, to considerable hoopla. Hundreds of plants were forced into bloom for display that March at the Philadelphia Flower Show, where they caused a huge stir. Edward R. Murrow even gave time to the gloriosa on his "Person-to-Person" television program. Well launched, these rudbeckias have since become a mainstay in many gardens.

Another rudbeckia, introduced earlier in this century in Germany by the eminent plantsman Karl Foerster, is one of the most widely planted perennials in the United States today. Called 'Goldsturm', it is notable for its toughness, drought-tolerance, prolific bloom from midsummer into autumn, and attractive seed heads in winter.

Like the gloriosa daisy, 'Goldsturm' has its story behind it—a story reinforcing the point that Europeans perceive possibilities in some of our North American native plants that we ourselves overlook. The tale of 'Goldsturm' begins in 1937, when Heinrich Hagemann, an apprentice to Karl Foerster, discovered a group of some sixty selected plants of *Rudbeckia fulgida* var. sullivantii in a botanical garden in Czechoslovakia. Deeply impressed, he told Foerster on his return that this rudbeckia was even better than Foerster's own favorite, *Rudbeckia fulgida* var. neumanii. Foerster doubted his assistant's claim, but encouraged him anyway to go back to Czechoslovakia to obtain plants. Hagemann did so (I suspect by more certain and direct means than asking for them), and he smuggled a few over the border in his backpack. The next summer, when the plants started blooming, Foerster summoned

Rudbeckia 'Goldsturm', for good reason, is one of the most widely planted perennials of the twentieth century, in Europe as well as in America, where its ancestors originated. It is a stalwart of the late summer and fall.

Hagemann and told him that he was right, these were the best rudbeckias he had ever seen. He added, however, that they needed a better name. Two days later he came up with 'Goldsturm'. The plants were then propagated by cuttings to build up stock. After the Second World War they began to circulate among German nurserymen and gardeners. In the 1960s and 1970s the plant spread to other European countries, arriving here in the late 1970s. It has since gone on to brighten many a garden and also to gladden the hearts of many people in the nursery trade, for whom it has been more of a gold mine than a gold storm.

'Goldsturm' does not quite exhaust the subject of German fascination with our native rudbeckias, although it has received the most press. From *Rudbeckia nitida*, a southeastern native, the Germans have selected a form called 'Herbstsonne' ('Autumn Sun'), which is lovely from August into October. It grows six or seven feet high and requires no staking. Its pale yellow flowers lack the harsh brown center of some other rudbeckias, and it may be left standing over the winter for its handsome seed heads.

SALVIAS

Gardening offers a lifelong series of chances to unlearn the things you thought you knew perfectly well, and I can't think of a better example of this principle than salvias. I thought I knew my salvias. I scoffed at most of them, the torrid red annual bedding sorts that pain the eye and made me long for a black freeze in early August, especially when they managed to consort with orange marigolds in a marriage that takes place far too often. I had a somewhat better opinion of the mealy-cup salvias, *Salvia farinacea* and its hybrids. The mealy-cups are far from spectacular, but they fill empty spaces in the border in a serviceable way, blooming from early summer to frost. Their spikes are light violet blue or a silvery white that looks attractive unless something truly white, like *Lavatera* 'Mont Blanc', is growing nearby. The white of the salvia then shows up as dingy by comparison.

In the last few years I've learned more about salvias, and learned about more salvias, enough to know that there's more learning to come. I also have a hunch that the genus is going to be one of the hot new tickets in American horticulture as we move into the twenty-first century.

All salvias have some traits in common. They all bear both flowers, which bloom fairly briefly, and bracts, which remain much longer, sometimes for months. All have the square stems and mouthlike flowers with clearly distinct upper and lower lips that mark them as members of the mint or Labiatae family. All bloom somewhat randomly, with new flowers and bracts continuing to form at various places up and down the flower stalk. Attractiveness to bees and, often, to hummingbirds is the rule. So is aromatic foliage, with scents ranging from sharp and pungent to more pleasant scents of grapes, citrus, and even honeydew melon.

But beyond their similarities begin their differences. Some salvias are staunchly dependable perennials in northern climates. Some are iffy, getting through one northern winter but not the next. A great many, the majority in fact, are tropical or subtropical perennials that behave like annuals in the temperate zone, having to be replanted each spring from seed or reproduced from cuttings taken from plants wintered over in greenhouses. Some salvias have rough-textured foliage, while others bear smooth, even waxy leaves. Some bloom briefly—and so late in the season that they qualify as true plants of autumn, not lingerers—but others are in almost continuous flower from early summer on. The range of color is large, extending from deep indigo and crystalline blue to fiery red, white, and even to yellow, as in the case of the forsythia sage (*Salvia maderiensis*) from Costa Rica.

Salvia guaranitica, *S. uliginosa*, *S.* 'Indigo Spires', and *S. coccinea*—with these four began my higher education concerning salvias, and they are still among my favorite autumn lingerers. A friend who heard me scoff at salvias one summer sent me small plants of each the next spring, and I was soon converted. The first two are large and shrubby, but no one could possibly confuse them with each other. *S. guaranitica* is not an especially generous bloomer, but the flowers are so much like gleaming sapphires that to see the plant is to want it. It also brings a splendid dividend: when from the corner of my eye I catch that bright flash of wings,

Salvia azurea 'Grandiflora' leans appealingly into a clump of fountain grass. Few plants of any season offer the superb blues of many of the late-flowering salvias.

that darting movement, that sudden hovering in space, I know that a hummingbird is visiting this salvia, which hummers seem to prefer to all other flowers.

A fit companion for *S. guaranitica* is *S. uliginosa.* Commonly known as bog sage, it nevertheless does well in my dry and well-drained soil. The flowers, borne on graceful, willowy stems, are Cambridge blue from a distance, but up close they prove to have much white around their throats, the entire blossom being crystalline, as if sprinkled with diamond dust. Both *S. guaranitica* and *S. uliginosa* have proved reliably hardy in my garden with the help of a deep mulch of salt hay and pine needles in early winter, although I suspect that I grow them near the northern limits of their winter hardiness.

My third salvia, a cultivar named 'Indigo Spires', is not reliably hardy in Zone 8, although I have known it to survive an especially mild winter in my own Zone 7 garden when heavily mulched with salt hay and shredded leaves. But it is easily obtainable in the spring from several mail-order nurseries, and northern gardeners with greenhouses can dig up and pot plants in mid-autumn. They will continue to bloom under glass through the winter, and new plants can be propagated from cuttings in early spring.

The first time I grew 'Indigo Spires', I had only one plant and lost sight of it when some surrounding tall artemisias and ornamental grasses overwhelmed it. That September, Hella waded through the tangle of vegetation and picked a few spikes to use in a bouquet with pink cosmos. Much impressed by the great length of the spikes, their loopy habit of growth, the true indigo of the blossoms that were open, and the blackish purple of the persistent calyces, I vowed never to go without this plant. I knew it was a salvia but didn't know which, thanks to bad memory, failure to make lists of new plants or maps of flower beds, and the incorrigible habits of an occasional visitor, a Scotch terrier named Cutty; he removes plastic plant labels and chews them to bits. I christened the plant *Salvia incognita,* but then the friend who gave it to me said it was 'Indigo Spires', a plant that originated in California as a chance hybrid between *S. farinacea* and *S. longispicata.*

The next year I ordered eighteen plants of 'Indigo Spires',

Top: The spikes of *Salvia uliginosa* twist and dance in the breeze, bringing movement as well as color to the garden. Bottom: *S.* 'Indigo Spires' in early September, just as its color starts to intensify and its spikes begin their weeks of dramatic elongation.

Even at the back of a small garden *Salvia guaranitica* pulls the composition together with its scintillating points of sapphire.

planting them in a sort of S-shaped river that wound its way from the front of a border well into its mid-ground. When the first spikes appeared in June, I was disappointed. 'Indigo Spires' was a bust. It wasn't indigo, for one thing, just a dull light violet blue. Its upright spikes were boring. It flowered generously and constantly, but it was still a plain Jane of a plant. I wondered if there had been a mistake. Had my friend been wrong about the name? Had the nursery sent the wrong plant?

The answer to both questions turned out to be no. The truth is that this salvia is unexciting for much of the summer. But in late August, as the light begins to change and the nights get cooler, 'Indigo Spires' undergoes a stunning transformation. The color of the flowers deepens and intensifies to true indigo. The spikes also elongate, becoming heavier and heavier. As they do, gravity overcomes their upright tendencies, producing the lateral and loopy habit I had so much admired the first year I grew this salvia. Strong winds and heavy rains in early September usually beat the plants down a bit, and some of the spikes begin to swoop or spiral loosely toward the earth, while others grow upward and out, assuming pendant shapes. Not only do its existing spikes elongate, but a great number of new ones form to triple their number, much increasing the show of color. By the time September ends, 'Indigo Spires' has become one of those plants that, like the ornamental grasses, are playthings of the wind, bringing to the garden a sense of movement and of choreography.

By late October, the spikes of 'Indigo Spires' have further intensified in color, and they have elongated to two feet long or more. Even on a still day, they are in constant motion from the weight of the bumblebees that come to rest on them or to drink their nectar. The spikes can also be dried for winter arrangements. The color fades to a less intense and somewhat metallic blue, but it is still attractive.

The final plant in my reeducation about the merits of salvias was *Salvia coccinea,* a native of woodlands near the coast of Texas, where it is perennial. North of Zone 9 it must be grown as an annual. It sometimes self-seeds, but to be safe I always order new plants in the spring from Well-Sweep or from Sandy Mush Herb

Salvia guaranitica.

Nursery. The flowers are as blazing a scarlet as any of the bedding salvias that I despise. The difference lies in the proportion between the tiny flowers and bracts of *S. coccinea* and its bright green foliage. The red is very bold and outspoken, but it is not overbearing, and it combines well with other colors, especially lavenders and pinks—and who would ever dream of using red bedding salvias with anything pink?

It would be monomaniacal, but it seems that it would be possible to have a garden of nothing but salvias. I hear rumors that there's a man in Greensboro, North Carolina, who grows almost three hundred species and cultivars. The Sandy Mush catalogue already offers well over sixty. Most of them are too tender to have much chance in my garden, but I don't have a great deal of space left for them anyway, so I've turned their tenderness into an advantage. Those that don't get through the winter I simply replace with new plants of new kinds. The annual investment is modest, typically $3 or so for a rooted cutting that can stretch anywhere between three and six feet tall by early fall. So far I have nothing but good words for those I've tried. *Salvia cardinalis* is a strong red, whose long flowers are much visited by hummingbirds. *S. Clevelandii* has sweet-smelling leaves and rich blue flowers. *S. urica* is another good blue. I will be trying many, many more.

Early in *The Graduate,* a businessman sidled over to utter a single word about the future to Dustin Hoffman's character: "Plastics." Were the time now, and if the fellow were a gardener, I think he'd whisper: "Salvias."

SAPONARIA

Ordinary *Saponaria officinalis,* or bouncing Bet, is not a desirable plant for a garden. Brought to North America by early British colonists for use in making soap, it was one of the first plants to escape from our gardens to our roadsides. It is equally willing to escape back from roadside to garden, where it is a great bully, seeding itself everywhere as well as spreading by underground stems. But one form of bouncing Bet, *S. officinalis* 'Rubra Plena', has better manners. It spreads a bit, but since it's sterile it won't

In Nancy Goodwin's garden at Montrose, in Hillsborough, North Carolina, early October sees a tapestry of perennial salvias and verbena, together with the highly ornamental buttery yellow blossoms of *Abelmoschus manihot,* a close relative of okra. This garden, seen here in only its first season after planting, is a swirl of colors both subtle and bright around the handsome urn.

pop up everywhere. From midsummer until October it keeps producing fluffy little double blossoms of baby-ribbon pink. It is also
sweetly fragrant, especially toward evening, when its delicious and
delicate scent can be detected from halfway across a garden. In *The
Fragrant Path* (1932) Louise Beebe Wilder placed it with night-
scented stock and sweet rocket as a "vesper flower"—one which
withholds its fragrance during the day and then richly bestows it
on the evening and nighttime hours. "Dowdy and forlorn," Mrs.
Wilder wrote, "this one-time belle appears by day, . . . [but] in the
twilight you will be surprised by her young freshness and the sweet
breath with which she will entice you."

STACHYS

Lamb's ears (formerly *Stachys lanata*, and still sold under that
name, but technically now *S. olympica* or sometimes *S. byzantina*)
is a plant with gray foliage so soft and downy that I'm always
tempted to rub it against my cheek—and sometimes do. (An old
common name for it is Quaker rouge, commemorating the former
practice of Quaker women who used the plant to bring a permissible blush to their faces when more frankly cosmetic substances
were shunned as frivolous.) It makes a good low ground cover that
spreads attractively but not in a troublesome way among other
perennials in a border. Although I enjoy the little towers of stems
in midsummer with their little magenta blossoms, some gardeners
would prefer not to have them, since they may produce a color
clash, should they be near something like the brilliant orange rose
'Cary Grant'. There is a form sold in England as 'Cotton Boll' and
in the United States as 'Sheila Macqueen', which produces flower
stalks but no flowers. Another form, entirely sterile, called 'Silver
Carpet', has given up even the slightest thought of sex and thus
remains low and spreading all year long.

Lamb's ears are especially lovely on frosty mornings, when
gleam is added to gray.

VERBENAS

The annual verbenas that garden centers sell every spring, usually in mixed colors from white to blazing red to dark purple, have their uses. They bring a great deal of flashy color to the garden, they stay short and tend to spread widely, they bloom over a long period, and they can take drought and heat. These are not inconsiderable virtues.

But my heart belongs to some perennial verbenas, even if I must in some instances put "perennial" in quotation marks to signal variable performance as regards winter hardiness. And in one case I must even put "verbena" itself in quotation marks. The botanical splitters, those who decide that species that used to be in the same genus are now in different ones, have decreed that *Verbena tenuisecta* is now *Glandularia tenuisecta.* I will balk here, on the grounds not only of long habit but also of conviction that glandularia sounds more like a disease than a plant. What I continue to call *V. tenuisecta* is a delicate creeping plant, with small clusters of lavender-blue flowers. (There is also a white form.) It may get through a mild winter in Zone 7, or it may not. One of the best uses of this verbena is to plant it in association with colchicums, to a fine result. Its carpet of finely dissected leaves provides a foil for the magnificent, vase-shaped pink blossoms of the colchicums when they flare forth in September, and the harmony of the colors is very satisfying. This verbena insinuates itself pleasantly into nearby plantings, as does *V. canadensis,* whose much larger clusters of flowers range from an almost electric pink to purple, against a background of foliage that takes on a purple cast as the temperatures begin to drop. *Verbena canadensis* can survive winters in Zone 6, but even in Zone 7 it's not a bad idea to put some cuttings in a cold frame, just in case.

Another fine verbena, a perennial in the Deep South but an annual farther north, is *V. peruviana,* which was collected in Peru and Brazil in the nineteenth century. Its clusters of clear, bright red flowers show up well from a great distance, like signal fires. The color is pure, without a trace of harshness.

All of these verbenas so far are low creepers. The Brazilian

Verbena canadensis, a low and prostrate plant, scrambles cheerfully among the stones of this rock garden in late September.

Tall and airy, *Verbena bonariensis*, seen here at the Arboretum of North Carolina State University in Raleigh, is an ideal scrim plant—one that can be planted at the front of a border without concealing the play of color in other plants behind it.

species *V. bonariensis* is, however, a much taller plant, growing as high as 4½ feet. It has an odd form, at once gaunt and spreading, with highly indented foliage and abundant little lavender-violet flowers. Like *Gaura lindheimeri,* it is a scrim plant that can be used near the front of a border, since its habit is open enough not to block sight of the plants behind it. The question of winter hardiness is vexing. Some people claim to grow *V. bonariensis* in Zone 4; others, in zones 5, 6, and 7, express their doubts. It may be one of those plants, iffy in nature and inconsistent from one year to the next, which are such good self-seeders that gardeners may know only that they've got *V. bonariensis* another year without knowing whether it's the same plant they had before.

One last perennial verbena, *V. rigida,* needs to be approached with some caution and probably should not be given a toehold in the garden. The seed catalogues describe it enticingly as a heat-tolerant, long-blooming plant that produces great sheets of silvery-blue flowers. Nancy Goodwin says it does indeed have fine color and blooms unstintingly. But once in the garden, it grows every-where it isn't wanted, and its stoloniferous roots are virtually im-possible to eradicate. Dynamite probably wouldn't help much. Nancy says that if some kind-hearted, generous soul offers me a start of *V. rigida,* I should smile, accept the gift, and then burn the plant. But Ann Lovejoy says the same plant has perfect manners in her garden on Bainbridge Island in Puget Sound. The lesson here is that when gardeners say that this plant or the other should be avoided as a troublemaker, the advice sometimes needs to be qualified—avoided in some parts of the country, in some gardens, under some conditions of soil and climate. What may gallop here may only romp there, and in some other place it may even sulk or pine away. But I'm sticking to Nancy's advice, leaving this verbena to other gardeners who as grownups still enjoy the game of chicken.

VIOLAS

Humanity's love of violets is as ancient as our love of roses and of irises. In Greek mythology, violets were created by Zeus as dainty food for the demigoddess Io after he made love to her and then changed her into a heifer to protect her from Hera's jealous rage. Early Christian symbolism found in the violet an image of the Trinity and of God's watchful eye over His creation. Violets have been candied and strewn on desserts, and there is now some vogue for putting them in salads. And starting late in the eighteenth century, hybridizers and collectors began messing around with them, mixing the species together, striving for new colors and forms, and most of all trying to turn flowers of modest size into jumbos and supersonics.

About violets I shall say fairly little, for violets do fairly little in the fall. There's one cultivar named 'Lianne' whose dark purple and very fragrant flowers begin in the autumn. *Viola odorata* 'Rosina' has wonderfully fragrant mauve to old-rose blossoms in both spring and fall, and sometimes will even produce a few flowers during mild spells in winter. The Labrador violet *(V. labradorica)* is fine in or out of bloom for its smoky purple foliage. But most species and cultivars of *Viola* produce only sporadic blossoms, if any, during this season.

The members of the genus *Viola* (apart from pansies or *V. x wittrockiana,* which are annuals) that qualify as lingerers are the violas. I know that this sounds confused. The reason that it sounds confused is that it is confused. Since the early nineteenth century, hybridizers working with *V. cornuta,* the horned violet of the Spanish Pyrenees, and with such other species as *V. tricolor,* the Johnny jump-up, have produced a great many long-blooming garden perennials, all called violas. Thus we speak of our violas and our violets and our pansies as three different kinds of plants, yet all three are in the genus *Viola,* capitalized and in italics. Violas, at

In a small patch of the enormous herbaceous border designed by Edith Eddleman for the Raleigh arboretum, *Viola* 'Blue Elf', *Ajuga* 'Burgundy Glow', *Heuchera* 'Palace Purple', and Japanese painted ferns make a pleasing picture together.

any rate, are best described as perennials with blooms intermediate in size between pansies and violets.

Violas are such pleasant plants that a few belong in every garden, where they are happy in the odd corner, but they have never inspired in me a great passion to collect them, as has happened at various points in my gardening life with irises, daylilies, astilbes, hostas, dianthuses, heaths and heathers, and sedums. I have some favorites. 'Arkwright Ruby', which blooms from April through early October, is a deep ruby red, blotched with dark brown. 'Blue Elf' is one of the most tenaciously blooming plants I know, flowering from late March to November. Edith Eddleman reports from North Carolina that she has had it in bloom from March through January. 'Lord Nelson' is in flower from May into late September. It has deep purple-violet blossoms, and it doesn't slow down during summer's heat as much as some other cultivars do.

Finally, there's 'Molly Sanderson', a real treasure and a terrific novelty. Its flowers, which appear nonstop from early April through the end of October, with a slight flagging in August, are black, black beyond any dispute, save for a slight flaring touch of gold and purple at the throat. No other plant described as having black flowers has ever quite lived up to its billing. 'Molly Sanderson' is black. Period. Set next to a piece of charcoal, it matches exactly. But what do you do with a black flower? Hella found the answer: you plant it in the middle of a spreading golden sheet of creeping Jenny or *Lysimachia nummularia* 'Aurea'. The black not only stands out but also becomes blacker, and the gold gets more golden. There is no lingerer more lovely than 'Molly Sanderson'.

Perennials Specific unto the Season

In late winter, gardeners spend a lot of time eagerly awaiting any sign of spring. This trait in us might be called the phenomenon of unsynchronous attention. When trees are bare and ice is underfoot, we long as ardently as Tristan for Isolde for the first snowdrops, the first sure promises that spring is about to happen, the thermometer and the wind-gauge notwithstanding. Snowdrops prophesy crocuses, and crocuses foretell tulips, daffodils, and all the rest of the flora of high spring. Together, tulips and crocuses are harbingers of an explosion of bloom and color beginning in April that will bring us once again to take possession of our gardens—and bring our gardens to take possession of us, body and soul, as we work the cool, clean-smelling earth and revel in its every gift to our senses.

I have come to respect the lingering perennials that make the autumn garden a continuation of what has been. But the true and special delight of autumn comes in the great numbers of plants that are specific to the season, those that withhold themselves until they and we are ready. I look forward as eagerly to the first appearance of Joe Pye weed in early August as I do to the first snowdrop in late winter. It too is a harbinger, but a harbinger of fall. I watch it emerge from the earth in May, gather strength to become a huge and noble presence in my garden as its sturdy and erect purple stems bear its long, rough leaves higher and higher. In the rich, moist soil it rises twelve, even fourteen feet tall by the first of August, calling to mind the story of Jack and the beanstalk. The buds begin to show about then, and they suddenly open into cumulus clouds of soft and misty pale purple. It is like the Bible's pillar of smoke by day, a beacon leading onward to a promised season, as much to be hoped for as any promised land.

Joe Pye weed is the beginning of a long parade of plants that start blooming late, some of which will keep it up until November. The garden in autumn becomes something new and fresh when the perennials peculiar to the season begin to flower, their time come round again at last. These plants, in which the onset of bloom is triggered by decreasing day length, have their own internal calendars. They know that autumn is here, and they tell us all about it.

ACONITUM

Commonly known as monkshood, for their helmeted blossoms somewhat resembling the cowl of a monastic robe, and known also as wolfsbane, for their traditional use to poison animals, sometimes including human ones, the aconites have a whiff of mystery and danger about them. The legends that have surrounded them since classical antiquity are distinctly unpleasant. Pliny the Younger wrote that when Hercules dragged the dog Cerberus from his spot guarding the entrance to Hades, it frothed at the mouth in rage, and the aconite sprang from its spittle. Alternatively, the plant came from the blood of Prometheus after eagles feasted on his liver. In medieval Christian iconography, the plant had only one symbolic meaning—death. From a purely scientific and chemical stand-point, the various monkshoods are in fact a source of highly toxic and potentially lethal compounds. For years, until our children were grown men, I was content to leave aconites to others. But I may have been overly cautious. Our older son, Paul, did have to undergo gastric lavage after eating a poisonous plant when he was two years old, but the culprit was the fruit of a Chinaberry tree in a neighbor's yard, not a monkshood. The fact is that such a great number of ornamental plants are poisonous—daffodils and fox-gloves, for starters—that a garden made up only of plants of assured innocence would be surpassingly dull. Once out of diapers, children seldom run around gardens munching experimentally on flowers and leaves, and they can early be taught to stick to food from the kitchen. As for monkshood, I suspect that if it were used, as is possible, in Renaissance Florence to help one's enemies depart ahead of schedule for the Next Life, it was slipped into food or drink in concentrated form, not served as a salad.

Some species of monkshood bloom in summer, not in the au-tumn, and there is much confusion over the correctness of the most commonly offered fall bloomer, *Aconitum carmichaelii,* sometimes listed parenthetically as *A. fischeri.* Occasionally, a catalogue will list both names separately, with no explanation of whether the same plant is listed under both names or two different plants are actually offered. To complicate the issue still further, a British friend has offered his judgment that the plants he has seen in America labeled as *A. carmichaelii* are no such thing at all, but something else. (What it is, he didn't say.) Whatever it is, the plant I grow under this name is lanky, growing to some four or five feet tall, with leaning tendencies. Tidy gardeners may want to stake it, but I just let it lean, making sure its neighbors are capable of offering it some support. Its dour blue-purple blossoms stand out especially well among pink Japanese anemones. Other worthy early fall bloomers are *A. x bicolor* (thought to be a hybrid between *A. napellus* and *A. variegatum*), 'Bressingham Spire', and 'Blue Sceptre'. Monks-hoods appreciate moist soil, a deep mulch, and partial shade. They tend to be short lived, and in regions where warm summer nights are common, they are plagued by fungus diseases. The distinctive form of their blossoms and their somber colors, however, make them well worth growing and replacing as needed.

ANEMONES

Anemones are a rich and varied genus of herbaceous or tuberous plants in the ranunculus family. Some bloom in the spring or early summer, but the handsomest of all, for their purity and grace and exceedingly clear colors, are the Japanese anemones—*Anemone hupehensis* var. japonica, *A. vitifolia,* and a large number of cultivars that as a group go under the name *A. x hybrida.*

These anemones were widely hybridized in Great Britain and the United States in the nineteenth and twentieth centuries, as well as in France by the Lemoines and in Germany by Wilhelm Pfitzer; such cultivar names as 'Géante des Blanches' and 'Prinz Heinrich' and 'Bressingham Glow' testify to their cosmopolitan careers. Collectively, they are known as Japanese anemones, but even *A. hupehensis* var. japonica itself is a misnomer. The British plant-explorer and botanist Robert Fortune collected it and other species not in Japan, but in China, where they are often planted in cemeteries for their lavish bloom in November. In *A Naturalist in Western China* (1913), E. H. Wilson, one of the greatest plant-collectors of all time, mentions that many plants thought to be of Japanese origin, including kerrias and these anemones, are actually part of the rich flora of China. Describing his journey through the Laolin Wilderness,

No autumn garden can be complete without the hybrid "Japanese" anemones that hail from China. 'Margarete' (left), a semidouble, has enormous panache and elegance. 'September Charm' (center) earns its name and then some. 'Alba', like the later-blooming cultivar 'Honorine Jobert', lends a calm and dignified note, especially near dusk, when the pristine white of its blossoms picks up the warm glow of the setting sun.

Wilson writes that "clearings and abandoned cultivated areas are overgrown with the handsome *Anemone vitifolia,* var. alba, which was 4 to 5 feet tall, and bore myriads of large attractive flowers. This herb made a wonderful display, and I do not remember having seen it so luxuriant elsewhere in my travels."

Despite the fact that we gardeners will probably persist in misspeaking of "Japanese" anemones halfway through the next millennium, more of us should grow them, under any name. They bloom for over a month, starting in very late summer or early autumn, and they make excellent, long-lasting cut flowers, provided that they are cut when they first begin to open, to prevent the

A large colony of *Anemone vitifolia* 'Robustissima' lights up a shady border at Nancy Goodwin's garden in North Carolina, growing in front of a boxwood hedge that was planted in the middle of the nineteenth century.

blossoms from shattering. Their color range extends from pristine white through clear pink to lavender mauve, but whatever their hue, the petals generally have a silvery cast and a silken look. Nursery catalogues offer several named varieties. Some, such as 'Mont Rose' and 'Queen Charlotte', are double or semidouble, but I prefer the singles, and two of them especially. 'September Charm' bears single clear pink flowers above lovely rich green foliage that is handsome all summer. The first flowers begin opening in late August, and the last petals drop in early October. The flower stalks, growing to four to five feet tall where they have the partial shade, moist soil, and deep mulching they need to grow best, can be left standing after bloom is over so you can enjoy the crop of seeds produced in white puffs, like little cotton bolls, in late October into November. 'Honorine Jobert', a later bloomer, is a fine pure white with foliage that takes on a bronze-purple cast in cool weather. It is one of my favorite plants of autumn—or any other season, for that matter—for its dignity and simple grace.

Not only are anemones beautiful, they are also tough once established. They grow equally well in upstate New York, where the winters are long and fierce, and in the North Carolina piedmont, where winter can be no trifling matter and where summers are long and torrid. But Japanese anemones take some care to get started. Small plants set out in the spring may not make much of a show at all the first year, but if they are coddled, then the patient gardener will be much rewarded by their spectacular bloom in years to come. No plant of autumn brings more joy than Japanese anemones. They look wonderful if given a spot all to themselves in front of shrubbery, but they also associate very well with ferns growing at their feet.

ASTERS

Americans often have to be taught to appreciate some of our native plants by our fellow gardeners across the Atlantic—and even then we can be slow learners. A prime example of perennials that have come back to our shores after their further education in England or Europe are the Michaelmas daisies, from programs of selected breeding using the common New England aster *(Aster novae-angliae)* as a jumping-off point. 'Treasurer', 'Alma Potschke', and others—they are all good, and the dark lavenders and purples among them fill out the cool end of the spectrum, nicely balancing the warmer tones that are common in garden chrysanthemums.

I have a favorite among the many cultivars of the Michaelmas daisy, a plant that enabled me to realize a dream long harbored—to enrich the gardens of friends and strangers alike by contributing something beautiful that otherwise might not be known and grown. I know nothing of its origins. It may have been developed in England, imported to the United States with a fancy name, sold in the nursery trade for a time, and then lost to commerce. Or someone in America may have selected a superior form of *A. novae-angliae.* I discovered it growing in a few neighborhood gardens in New Jersey when we moved here in 1972. When I first clapped eyes on it in a front yard just down the block, I knew it was classy. This aster is very sturdy, requiring no staking, although it grows up to four feet high and the same distance across. It bears enormous numbers of large, single, purple flowers, each with a bright golden

Aster 'Hella Lacy' (left), which I discovered in my neighborhood years ago and named for my wife, was introduced recently by several perennial nurseries. *Aster* 'Harrington's Pink' (right), an old-timer, fairly sparkles on a clear cool day.

eye when it first opens. For the two weeks that it stays in bloom, starting in mid- to late September, it is the handsomest plant in town, not only for its intensity of color but also for the great numbers of Monarch butterflies hovering over it and lighting on its flowers to sip nectar.

Such a plant is not to be kept to oneself. It had no name that I knew of, so years ago I began sending it out to gardening friends all across the country, asking if they knew what it was. No one knew, but everyone wrote back that they loved it as much as I did. Several nurseries wanted to propagate and sell it, but they wanted a name. I named it 'Hella Lacy'. Like all the cultivars of the New England aster, this one tends to lose its lower leaves during especially dry summers if allowed to reach its full height. One remedy is to cut it back by half in mid-June. Another is to surround it with lower growing perennials that will conceal its naked ankles. It gets on especially well with crocosmia 'Lucifer' for people who have not outgrown their grade school affection for drawing with orange-red and purple crayons. The spiky foliage of crocosmias and their somewhat jagged stems lend a note of textural interest.

Not long ago, a nurseryman friend who offers 'Hella Lacy' sent me another aster to try out—*A. lateriflorus* 'Horizontalis'. It came from West Germany, he said. No question about it—this aster is one of the great joys of the autumn garden. It grows under eighteen inches high with a spread of two feet. In full bloom it looks like a mauve-colored mist. Its blossoms are small, under half an inch across, but they are wonderfully constructed. The disk flowers at their center are little pompoms the color of ripe raspberries, and the ray flowers are white and slightly bent back. Its loveliness is subtle, not dramatic; it speaks softly, rather than screaming to be noticed. Even on a first-year plant, the blossoms number in the hundreds, and the tiny, bronze-purple leaves lend an additional touch of beauty. I like this aster very much indeed, but it turns out to be no more German than turkey and cranberry sauce. It's a North American native whose range extends from southeastern Canada across to Minnesota and then down to parts of Texas and Florida. I've probably seen it a jillion times along roadsides without paying any heed, but now that it's in my garden, by way of Ger-

Signs of the season: *Aster* 'Hella Lacy', in our garden near the coast of southern New Jersey, plays host to migrating monarch butterflies en route to their winter home in central Mexico.

many, where horticulturists have selected 'Horizontalis' for its spreading form, its virtues are clear. Here is just one more example of the debt Americans owe to Europeans for their keen appreciation of perennials whose familiarity in the wild blinds us to their potential loveliness in the garden.

Are there other native asters worth inviting into the perennial border? The answer is a resounding yes. I can't imagine anyone saying unkind words about *A. cordifolius,* whose common names include bee weed and bee tongue. From its heart-shaped basal leaves, it sends up sprays 2½ feet tall, bearing blossoms with pale lavender ray flowers and disk flowers that start out yellow and then turn purple. It is handsome planted with one of the tall goldenrods, such as *Solidago sempervirens,* a combination that deliberately repeats an association common in the wild. Another native aster, much appreciated in Great Britain and well worth growing, is *A. divaricatus,* a front-of-the-border plant with starry white flowers and wiry black stems up to twenty-four inches tall. *A. ericoides,* whose common name is heath aster for its heathlike foliage, also produces an abundance of white stars. Since it reaches thirty-six inches, it may be grown near *A. divaricatus* to echo the color and size of the latter's flowers on a plant of more generous proportions. A cultivar of *A. ericoides* called 'Esther' that grows to about eighteen inches produces graceful wands bearing a multitude of small, pale pink blossoms. Another worthy aster is *A. linearifolius,* the

In this mid-October scene in the Raleigh arboretum, tall *Aster tataricus* (left), a champion for its long season of bloom, mingles handsomely with *Solidago sempervirens* and *Salvia leucantha. Aster lateriflorus* 'Horizontalis' (right) covers itself with myriads of tiny flowers.

bristly aster, which grows just a foot high and produces bright violet flowers, occasionally in bunches but usually singly at the top of each stem, above delicate and narrow leaves.

Edith Eddleman is partial to *A. patens.* It has very large purple-blue flowers some 2½ inches across, borne on four-foot stems that curve down toward the ground. In her perennial border at the Raleigh, North Carolina, arboretum, I saw it used with white frost asters *(A. pilosus)* and some pale raspberry double chrysanthemums. When I commented that *A. patens* sprawled a bit, Edith set me straight right away. A plant that sprawls, she said, falls prostrate and crushes other plants. *A. patens* "just curves or bends down gracefully, like Robert Frost's birches. It's a very nice combination," she added, "blue arching down over raspberry and white." The same arching habit is found in a decidedly blue aster that Nancy Goodwin found growing in an old southern garden and named 'Our Latest One' to rescue it from anonymity.

There is great fun, I think, in sitting down before a stack of nursery catalogues in hope that some long-desired plant or other will turn up, but for readers who prefer some other way of occupying their time, I offer a hint as a shortcut. With one exception, Canyon Creek Nursery, Montrose Nursery, and Sunlight Gardens manage among them to offer all the native asters I have mentioned.

Aster frikartii 'Mönch', bred in Switzerland shortly after World War I, now enjoys widespread distribution in both Europe and North America. I find it indispensable. It has a long period of bloom beginning in midsummer.

The exception is *A. pilosus.* It is a common weed along eastern roadsides, and it self-seeds so prodigiously that bringing it into a garden is an act of considerable courage.

Not all the asters bred on the other side of the Atlantic and readily available here have a North American ancestry, of course. The truly indispensable *Aster x frikartii* 'Mönch', a rich blue that blooms over a long period starting during the summer, was hybridized in the 1920s at the Frikart nursery in Switzerland. It is a cross between *A. amellus,* native to Italy, and *A. thompsonii,* from the Himalayas. Another alien aster I would not want to be without is native to Siberia and Mongolia, its range extending southward into China and Korea. It is the tatar aster, *A. tataricus.* It has certain faults, being somewhat ungainly at seven feet or more, with the flowers bunched together atop the lanky stems. But its single blossoms are a fine pale blue, and its season of bloom stretches longer and later than that of any aster I know, extending from late September until early November. I have seen the tatar aster used very handsomely, planted in a mass at the edge of a meadow. Even from a distance, it is showy and fetching.

Aster cordifolius 'Silver Spray', growing with tall anemones in Cynthia Woodyard's garden in Portland, Oregon.

BEGONIA GRANDIS

I use the annual wax begonias generously to fill in blank spots in the garden, both in full sun and in partial shade, and I always manage to have a few of the wonderfully colored tuberous begonias growing in pots in the shade. I treat these tender plants as annuals, not wanting to go through the bother of saving the tubers over the winter. But my favorite garden begonia is a perennial. It blooms much less freely than wax begonias, and its flowers can claim only quiet charm, not the gaudy magnificence of its tuberous kin. Once called *Begonia evansiana,* and still listed under that name in many nursery catalogues, it is now *B. grandis.* The name seems not to fit. *Grandis* in Latin means large, but nothing about the plant is at all remarkable in size. It grows, in my garden at least, only about fifteen inches tall. The leaves do not exceed six inches at most, and the flowers aren't much larger than those of the wax begonia, nowhere near approaching those of the tuberous begonia. Its common name, hardy begonia, is fairly reassuring, but it looks so delicate of constitution that I always mulch my plants deeply in late autumn and then watch nervously the next spring to see if they have made it through the winter. They are slow starters, coming up as late as mid-May from the roots and from tiny bulbils formed in the leaf axils the previous year, so the wait is an anxious one.

Begonia grandis is a true plant of autumn, not a lingerer like its kin. It begins to bloom in mid-September, keeping it up about one month. At first glance, it has only an understated beauty. The somewhat lobed leaves are olive drab. The flowers generally are a soft rose pink, translucent and slightly frosted, like satin glass. I also grow a white form, but it is something of a rarity. The great surprise is the undersides of the leaves. In the commoner rose-pink form they are a deep and solid kidney red. The white form is even more striking, with blood-red veins against a soft olive background. If placed where it catches the last low rays of the sun from behind, *B. grandis* offers a sight that is one of the epiphanies of autumn.

BOLTONIAS

Boltonia asteroides has only recently come to be recognized as a splendid garden perennial as well as a handsome roadside wild-flower. I grow two cultivars, and like them much for their slightly waxy, blue-gray foliage and their combination of delicacy and substantial presence. One is a selection called 'Snowbank'—an appropriate name, given the pure white single daisies it bears in huge numbers. It blooms for about three weeks starting in early September, on plants three to four feet tall that in full sun spread to five feet across. In partial shade, it is less assertive. The other, introduced by Montrose Nursery, is 'Pink Beauty'. It far exceeds 'Snowbank' in the size of its flowers and in the length of its season of bloom. The leaves are also a much richer shade of blue than those of 'Snowbank'. It stands four feet high by midsummer, starts blooming in early August, and doesn't call it quits until the first or second week of October. The soft pink of its flowers, each about the size of a quarter, combines well with grays and blues and purples. In a part of my back garden where I casually stuck 'Pink

In the early morning light in Nancy Goodwin's garden, *Boltonia* 'Pink Beauty' intensifies in color, taking on distinct tones of mauve and lavender.

Beauty' during the rush of spring planting the first year I had it, serendipity struck in one of those purely accidental combinations of forms and colors which are also so purely wonderful that they must be recreated deliberately in years to come. In this corner of the garden, artemisia 'Silver King' romped together with the pastel blue *Eupatorium coelestinum,* fighting it out for territory. Somehow or other, a seedling of the red annual salvia, *S. coccinea,* managed to push its way higher, punctuating all the gray and the blue with little scarlet exclamation points. Behind this melee, a single tall clump of *Boltonia* 'Pink Beauty' rose in quiet and dignified splendor, right next to an even taller specimen of the annual *Nicotiana sylvestris,* a huge cone of a plant, with its lowest leaves almost two feet long and with an explosion of pure white tubular flowers at its top. The rich variation in plant forms, leaf textures, and light or pastel colors, given a bit of spice by the scarlet of the salvia, lingered in the mind long after it was no longer present to the eye.

Both boltonias have lovely golden-tinted late fall foliage.

Boltonia 'Pink Beauty', punctuated by the tiny blossoms of *Salvia coccinea,* like little points of flame, in my garden in October.

Sturdy plants, they can be left standing over the winter for their interesting forms and the contrast they offer to ground covered with snow.

CHRYSANTHEMUMS

No plants are more associated with autumn in our imaginations than garden chrysanthemums, which most people insist on calling "mums," despite the frowns and strictures of purists who want to hear all four syllables roll from our lips. One of the great rituals of the season, even among people who garden only in the most minimal way, is a trip to a local garden center or even to a grocery store or a K-Mart to pick out several potted mums to flank their front doors or to brighten corners where little else may be in flower. Our florists have contrived it that we may also have potted mums for St. Valentine's Day or any other day of the year, but they strike me as inappropriate out of their true season, which is late summer and early autumn, when the nights have lengthened sufficiently to trigger the initiation of flower buds.

These chrysanthemums are among the most ancient of all ornamental perennials, even though they did not reach European and North American gardens in any quantity until the middle of the nineteenth century, during the great heyday of plant collection in the Far East by western botanists and horticulturists. We are Johnny-come-latelies in our admiration for chrysanthemums. They were cultivated in China in 500 B.C., a few years before the birth of Socrates and the rise of Athenian civilization to its brief glory, and they grew in Japanese gardens by the eighth century A.D.

It is easy to understand the widespread affection people have for their garden mums. They can be transplanted in bud or in full flower. Their range of color is immense, embracing white, pink, lavender, purple, apricot, gold, yellow, and something close to true red. Only blue is missing, and some of the Michaelmas daisies and other asters fill this gap handsomely. The form of the chrysanthemums' flowers is also diverse: there are singles, doubles, pompoms, buttons, as well as types with spidery or quilled or spoon-shaped petals. Their sharply aromatic foliage has a pleasing scent, as bracing as a cool, clear morning in mid-September. Because they can be purchased when in full bloom, gardeners know exactly what they are getting, with one important exception: it is impossible to tell from looking at a potted mum whether it will survive the winter and come back in the spring. Some of the large wholesale nurseries that grow chrysanthemums for retail outlets sell not only hardy sorts but also the tender cultivars developed for the florist industry and suitable only for growing in greenhouses in cold weather. But with these potted mums, it isn't necessary to wait until spring to get the bad news. If a plant hasn't formed a basal rosette of new leaves shortly after it finishes blooming, it will not be winter hardy in cold climates.

The potted mums that do not return may be something of a blessing in that those that do survive will have multiplied beyond the capacity of most gardens to absorb in the following year. The survivors need to be severely dealt with in late spring. When the new shoots reach about six inches high, a few can be pulled up, with a little bit of root attached, and then pinched back sharply and planted directly in the soil, where they will quickly form new roots and begin to branch from the base. Treated this way, chrysanthemum cuttings are splendid to fill in gaps in a herbaceous border or to conceal the ripening foliage of spring bulbs. The old clumps from which the cuttings are taken are best discarded. They will bloom, but with a crowded look reminiscent of a packed subway car at rush hour.

Although an autumn garden composed only of chrysanthemums would be a failure of imagination, a garden without them would be impoverished.

The easy availability of potted mums to make an instant autumn garden is a boon to lazy gardeners like me, but there are
disadvantages in this convenience: too few of us explore better ways
of coming by our chrysanthemums. Huff's Garden Mums and other
specialized nurseries, as well as more general nurseries like White
Flower Farm and Wayside Gardens, ship young plants in the
spring. The catalogues often indicate a rough date for the onset of
bloom, so that by careful selection the chrysanthemum season can
be extended from the middle of August until the end of October—
or even later in places where winter does not arrive early and
abruptly. Some chrysanthemums may even be grown from seed, as
perennials that will bloom in their first year. I mean here primarily
the Korean hybrids, developed by American breeders in the 1930s.
The best of these bear large single flowers in a wide range of warm
colors. Park sells seeds of these strains. The resulting plants will
vary considerably in garden merit, but it is easy to rogue the crop
after they bloom, selecting the very best and composting the others.
I like to grow these mums with little or no pinching back during
the summer, so that they assume a graceful and arching habit of
growth, producing flowers in sprays rather than in tight clumps. So
treated, they can be allowed to weave among other plants to form
a tapestry. To see these Korean mums grown and displayed at their
very best, gardeners who happen to be in Manhattan in mid-
October should visit the Conservatory Garden in Central Park.

One useful tip, for people who may resent the space chrysanthemums take up in a border before they start to bloom, is that they
may be grown in containers in a nursery area of any garden large
enough to permit this convenient amenity. Home-grown potted
mums can as easily be transplanted in full bloom where they are
wanted as those from K-Mart or the local garden center.

There are other chrysanthemums besides mums that are well
worth growing. The genus is a large one, with many species or
cultivars that no one would dream of calling mums. Feverfew, or
Chrysanthemum parthenium, a summer-blooming, short-lived perennial native to Europe, is one example. The complex hybrids
making up the Shasta daisies are also in the genus. So is the
Montauk daisy or *C. nipponicum,* a shrubby and somewhat woody

perennial with attractive glossy green foliage that persists through the winter in milder climates. The Montauk daisy bears large white flowers much resembling single Shasta daisies in late autumn—and may not bloom at all north of Zone 7.

Another species—a "new old" plant, meaning that it has just recently entered the nursery trade, although for some years it has passed through noncommercial channels from one gardener to another—is *C. pacificum.* It may not bloom reliably much north of Philadelphia, again because it is a very late bloomer. It almost doesn't matter. The buds are pleasant enough, little golden buttons

A summer bloomer in much of the country, feverfew *(Chrysanthemum parthenium)* continues flowering well into autumn in Ann Lovejoy's garden near Seattle, Washington. Here it combines elegantly with *Artemisia* 'Powis Castle' and *Senecio cineraria* 'White Dream'.

that look a bit like the buds of ageratums, but the flowers are insignificant. The real merit of this plant lies in its foliage. The dark green leaves are edged in silver. This native Japanese species makes a fine spreading ground cover about a foot high. Because it grows very well in sandy soils, as well as in heavier ones, it is a good plant for the seaside garden.

My favorite of all chrysanthemums, however, is *C. arcticum.* I'm not entirely certain if I have its name right, but that's what a friend who got a specimen from the late Elizabeth Lawrence said it was. It's another of those chrysanthemums which bloom so late that they may fail to bloom where winters come early. But in my garden it's one of the marvels of late fall, staying in bloom for three weeks at least, starting the end of October. It is a very silvery white single daisy on graceful, wiry stems. The buds are pink, and the back of the petals have a faint pink cast. It has superb foliage throughout the growing season—slightly cut, very fresh, and shiny bright green leaves. *C. arcticum* has one fault worth mentioning: it spreads aggressively, almost to the point of viciousness, especially in light soils. I am willing to overlook this fault, as I overlook faults in myself and in some close friends who fall short of perfection. If we ever move to someplace else and start another garden, *C. arcticum* will be one of some ten plants that will ride with us in the car to our new home. The only commercial source I know for it is Montrose Nursery.

CIMICIFUGAS

Beginning in midsummer with *Cimicifuga racemosa,* the cimicifugas have pride of place as one of the noblest American wildflowers. Their elegant beauty continues into autumn when *C. racemosa* bursts into bloom along back roads, where woodlands come almost to the pavement's edge. Growing up to seven feet tall, these plants bear long and narrow cylindrical spikes of creamy white florets on stems that branch like a candelabrum. They light up shady spots with all the drama of rockets or roman candles, the flowers lasting for weeks above large and ferny leaves. Splendid grown singly as an accent in a somewhat shaded perennial border, they are even more stunning grown as they often appear in the wild, in great masses or colonies. They perform best when given ample moisture. The variety 'Atropurpurea' grows only to three feet but can be highly recommended for its later season of bloom, in October, and for its handsome purple foliage. A new cultivar, 'Brunette', developed in Germany, has been highly touted for its even darker foliage. A few American nurseries are selling it at unbelievably high prices. But this plant is best avoided until such time as it can be propagated by tissue culture, as the existing stock of it has been discovered to be infected with harmful nematodes best not imported into gardens, where they can spread to other plants.

Cimicifugas have one defect worth noting—a distinctly unpleasant smell testified to in their common name, bugbanes. They are accordingly best planted in a distant corner—a good location to begin with, since they show up so magnificently from afar.

CLEMATIS

I am of several minds about the one clump of *Clematis heracleifolia* 'Davidiana' that hogs up a lot of room in our front garden. Nursery catalogues list it as thirty-six inches high, but it has to be staked to keep it even reasonably upright. It sprawls and slouches in such an uncouth way that when I look at it I sometimes hear my Grandmother Lacy's sharp injunction when I was in my early teens: "Allen, watch your posture!" Its leaves are coarse, and they burn and curl in hot, dry weather. But it still has its merits. The hyacinthlike clusters are intense blue-lavender, a welcome color in late August and into September. They have a powerful fragrance.

As for other clematis, they are properly or technically woody plants, or maybe semiherbaceous, but they aren't entirely out of place in a discussion of the plants of fall. Some of them are true fall bloomers. For starters, there's the sweet autumn clematis. Native to Japan but naturalized at the fringes of woodlands in the eastern United States, this vigorous vine loves to climb into shrubbery and small trees. There it drapes itself, producing frothy masses of small, creamy white, cruciform flowers with a delicious vanilla scent in late August and early September.

The buds and flowers of *Clematis tangutica* nod among the foliage like graceful parasols. The late-blooming clematises are one of the pure joys of autumn.

This particular clematis is a source of great vexation, although the plant is not at fault. I learned its scientific name as *Clematis paniculata*, eight syllables with a lovely euphony. Only reluctantly did I go along with those of my friends who are sticklish in matters nomenclatural in calling it *C. maximowicziana*. Now I am simply confused. Allen Paterson, director of the Royal Botanical Garden at Hamilton, Ontario, which in the last five years has assembled what may be the world's largest collection of clematis species and cultivars (more than five hundred kinds), says that the name, honoring the nineteenth-century Russian botanist Karl Ivanovich Maksimovich, has now been muscled aside. He says that to make

taxonomists happy, gardeners have got to learn to call the sweet autumn clematis *C. digitata.* But there's no agreement about this question among the British experts on clematis. The revised edition of Christopher Lloyd's book *Clematis* (1989) sticks with *C. maximowicziana.* Barry Fretwell's book, *Clematis* (1989), offers this comment: "If ever a plant suffered from the unwelcome attentions of the horticultural academics, this must come near the top of the list." Fretwell adds that it's also been known as *C. dioscoreifolia* var. robusta, mentions that he considers it a somewhat larger-flowered form of *C. flammula,* and himself calls it *C. ternifolia.* For now, I'll stick with "sweet autumn clematis."

Clematis 'Ville de Lyon', bred in France in 1899 as a hybrid of *C. texensis* and an unknown garden variety, blooms heavily in early summer and then again in September.

Autumn has other vining clematis that present no similar nomenclatural puzzlements. 'Lady Betty Balfour', a large-flowered purple hybrid with reddish overtones, blooms from September to late October. So do 'Ernest Markham', a fine red, and 'Mme. Baron Veillard', a lilac pink. *C. tangutica* and *C. orientalis* are notable for their multitude of nodding little yellow blossoms and their little whirlwinds of fuzzy-looking seed heads. *C. texensis*, one of several species native to Texas, and its cultivars 'Duchess of Albany' and 'Gravetye Beauty' are notable for their bell-like red to rose flowers and their allure to hummingbirds. *C. lasiandra*, a robust climber, has charming little tubular flowers striped pinkish purple and greenish.

Many other clematis will bloom in the fall, without being restricted to that season. Some blossom heavily in early summer, and then sporadically into late September or even October. These include 'Henryi', a very large single white with creamy tones; 'Mrs. Cholmondeley', a nice lavender-blue with darker veins; and 'Niobe', a fairly new hybrid, almost red-black at first, then fading to ruby. Other clematis blossom very heavily in May and June, rest during July and August, and then come back with a good show in September. Two favorites among these are 'Duchess of Edinburgh', a double white that sometimes bears lime-green sepals at the center of its flowers in cool weather, and 'Nelly Moser', a rose-mauve with more intense color along the center of its sepals and a lighter tone at their edges, to give a tricolor effect. Pruning any of the clematis that bloom in both summer and fall, with or without a resting period in between, can significantly increase autumn flowering, although the price paid will be scanty bloom or no bloom at all in early summer. The trick is to take a deep gulp in mid-March, cut back the vines sufficiently to feel aghast at the deed, and see to it that the plants get a heavy dose of fertilizer in midsummer and deep and regular irrigation.

There are three ways of growing clematis that are especially appealing. One is to plant them a foot or so from the trunk of a small tree, so that they will drape themselves through its outer branches in graceful swags. Among the best of trees for this purpose is quince, which stays just under eight feet and spreads in a wide dome shape. 'Lady Betty Balfour' is the clematis to use, since its rich purple combines dashingly with the greenish gold of the ripening fruit. Clematis may also be trained on the circular metal plant stakes that are so useful for supporting gypsophila and other floppy perennials. The stakes, which are about two feet in diameter, should be pushed firmly into the ground so that their tops stand thirty inches high. The vine will completely hide the metal, to form a pleasing mound that will surprise anyone who only thinks of clematis as a trellis plant. Finally, I have seen clematis trained up thick wooden stakes in herbaceous borders, to lend a fairly splendid narrow vertical accent, much in the manner of pillar roses.

EUPATORIUM

Allen Bush tells an amusing tale about a eupatorium. At the end of a visit to Bressingham Gardens, Alan Bloom's perennial nursery in England, he bought a plant to bring back to the United States for trial—"a very special eupatorium indeed," Bloom had called it. Always on the lookout for plants with special qualities, Bush went through all of the rigamarole needed to import this eupatorium, washing every speck of soil from the roots, having the plant inspected for disease or insects, and securing the permit that would get it past the United States Department of Agriculture's officials when he flew home.

"This eupatorium looked to me very much like plain old *Eupatorium purpureum,* one of the two species that goes by the common name Joe Pye weed," Bush says. "It's so common that few people would think of planting it in their gardens. But Alan Bloom had called it special, and he knows perennials as well as anyone on earth, so I planted it with great expectations." When it bloomed, it looked just like plain old Joe Pye weed. But the lesson of this tale is not that Alan Bloom's eupatorium turned out to be indistinguishable from a common American roadside weed. It is, instead, that this tall and commanding roadside weed deserves our respect and a place in our gardens.

Why do American gardeners give this plant so little attention? I think it must be that common name, Joe Pye weed. As regards

The smoky tones of lythrum, ornamental grasses, and Joe Pye weed make the yellow of the rudbeckias in the distance all the brighter. Although Americans have paid little court to our native Joe Pye weed or to our many species of goldenrod, our British cousins treat them as the royalty of the late-season garden.

the "Joe Pye" part of the name, there are two theories. One holds that in colonial times an Indian medicine man named Joe Pye cured typhoid fever and other ailments with a ghastly tasting tea brewed from the plant's leaves. The other theory is that in one of the American Indian languages *jopi* was the word for typhoid. Whatever the case, Joe Pye weed has no place in modern medicine, not at the moment anyway, although new medical uses for old herbs sometimes pop up in pharmaceutical research.

It is the "weed" part of the name that probably keeps us from bringing Joe Pye weed into our gardens. Considering crab grass, nut grass, chickweed, ragweed, and all the other vegetative menaces that keep us busy during their long seasons of growth, the hesitation about deliberately planting anything called a weed is understandable. Nevertheless I grow Joe Pye weed, and I love it. I wish I could say that I saw it growing on the roadside and was so struck by its dignified height and its subtle color that genius inspired me to invite it into my garden. It didn't happen that way. I saw it in a friend's garden. The genius was entirely hers. I was just a copycat.

The Joe Pye weeds of the roadside and those of the garden seem almost to be different plants entirely, but they aren't. Culture makes the difference. In the wild, where it often grows in dry soil of low fertility, the plant may grow anywhere between two and six feet tall. In fertile, moist garden soil, it easily reaches ten feet or more. Its purple-tinged stems are narrow and straight, and they are topped with clusters of lustrous pearly pink buds that open into tiny fringed blossoms the color of crushed raspberries. In my garden, a colony of Joe Pye weed begins to bloom early in August, by which time they have risen to twelve feet tall, looming over a large section of border, although they are planted well at the back, twenty feet from its front edge. The very large clusters of flowers have a billowy look, like the immense thunderheads of cumulonimbus clouds so often building up on the horizon in late afternoon at this time of year. Joe Pye weed blooms for a month at least. Its soft color and its monumental stature combine to make it a dramatic accent in the early autumn garden, and it is splendid in mixed bouquets.

Besides its beauty, there's one more reason to grow this plant.

It is aggressive, but the slightly shaggy little button flowers of the hardy ageratum *(Eupatorium coelestinum)* are always welcome in early autumn. For its drought resistance, this plant is one of the stalwarts of the sandy garden.

In my part of the country, as elsewhere, real estate developers are gobbling up land at a furious rate, and shopping centers, condominiums, and residential subdivisions are springing up everywhere. Joe Pye weed and some equally attractive native perennials, such as ironweed, are losing their habitats. A gardener's love may be a saving love that preserves plants worth keeping.

At first glance, except that its flowers are a dusty shade of white, boneset or *E. perfoliatum* much resembles Joe Pye weed. A closer look, however, reveals the distinguishing characteristic that gives this species its name. The two opposing leaves on each side of the hairy stem grasp it in such a way that it appears to pierce its way through their embrace. Growing to some six feet in height, this eupatorium associates well in the garden with its better-known kin.

The eupatorium most often found in gardens is *E. coelestinum*, the hardy ageratum. Its common name is misleading, for it's not an ageratum at all, although it bears a striking resemblance. A wildflower of the eastern seaboard, it has solid merit. It emerges late enough in spring to be a good cover for daffodils and other bulbs. In my garden it has proved remarkably immune to insect damage and disease, although in the South, where summer nights are warmer, it is susceptible to mustard-seed fungus. Drought hardly fazes it; it may wilt a bit in a rainless August, but the foliage freshens up when the first rains of September come and its month or more of bloom begins. It tolerates neglect, and the soft blue flowers in fluffy clusters are welcome when they appear.

Like its relative Joe Pye weed, the hardy ageratum alters its character when planted in a garden with moist and fertile soil. The change is not entirely benign. Under favorable conditions, it gallops and romps everywhere, spreading by underground stems with such vigor that it can swamp less aggressive plants. Some gardeners segregate it, placing it in a dry, out-of-the-way corner, where its vice can be a virtue, making it an effective ground cover growing about eighteen inches tall. Grown with other plants, it seems easy to eradicate, as it pulls up with no resistance. I try to get rid of it in one border every spring, but I always miss a few sprigs, and by late summer it is back in force. When it blooms I'm happy that I didn't succeed in exterminating it.

'Cory', a selected form of *E. coelestinum*, combines perfectly with the native American willow-leafed sunflower, *Helianthus salicifolius*.

The latest of all the eupatoriums to bloom, extending the season well into November, is *E. rugosum.* It looks much like a white form of hardy ageratum, except that it grows to three feet and bears much looser clusters of flowers on a plant with a more open and spreading habit. The flowers look to the naked eye like off-white balls of fluff, but seen through a hand lens they are wonderfully complicated, a mass of twisted petals arranged in a star shape. This species is commonly called sanicle, and it is one of several different native plants known as snakeroot, for its supposed ability to counteract the venom of rattlesnakes and copperheads. It is one of the best perennials I know for adaptability to dry shade. Sanicle is rather a pretty thing, but it has a dark history. *Human Poisoning from Native and Cultivated Plants,* by James W. Hardin and Jay M. Arena, reports that it poisons livestock and that humans have died from drinking milk contaminated with it.

The most wonderful of all eupatoriums is *E. capillifolium.* It bears the unlovely common name of dog-fennel, for reasons I cannot understand. I first saw it growing wild in Chincoteague, Virginia, one September. I had no idea what it was, but I did know that it was handsome in the extreme, a feathery and ferny thing that moved in the wind most attractively. Shortly after I identified it with a botanical key to eastern native plants, I received the latest catalogue from Niche Gardens, a wildflower nursery that grows its own plants rather than collecting them in the wild. Niche's co-owner, Kim Hawks, described dog-fennel in all the detail that comes from loving attention and keen observation. Its foliage is

interesting in all seasons. In the spring the narrow stems are densely covered with vibrant green threadlike leaves. These stems grow into a stunning fine textured 8–12′ vertical shaped multi-stemmed plant that commands attention as its stately, feathery, lush green stems sway in the slightest summer breeze. In the fall the habit of the plant becomes more pendulous and open as the foliage takes on a light green cast created by the individually inconspicuous white flowers. From the late fall until the spring flush of growth, the brown, dried stems look attractive moving in the wind.

In the Raleigh arboretum, dog fennel *(Eupatorium capillifolium)* erupts in October to produce hundreds of delicate little blossoms on feathery spikes or boas that glisten as they move in the wind. The plant is lovely indeed, but bears watching lest it make itself too much at home.

When covered with frost or snow, the stems sparkle and glisten. This native is extremely underused, and the texture is hard to replace with any other plant.

Kim Hawks was impressed by *E. capillifolium,* and I by her remarks. In Chincoteague, where it made a much smaller plant, I had considered trying it in my garden. This catalogue description made it sound like something that no one could possibly resist. But I had some questions. Would it be hardy north of Virginia's Eastern Shore? Even more important, would it be *too* hardy, one more in a long list of invasive plants like *Macleaya cordata* and *Oenothera speciosa* that I have invited into my plot to my lasting regret?

I asked some questions. Several people expressed astonishment that I could even think of planting such a horribly pushy plant. It would seed itself everywhere, they warned, and I would never be rid of it. They said I'd be better off planting ragweed. But other people, including Kim Hawks, assured me that this eupatorium had impeccable manners in a garden. There was a great mystery here. How could a plant be an angel one place, a devil someplace else?

A botanist friend supplied a convincing answer. All eupatoriums are members of the aster group in the composite family, a group in which self-sterility is common. Self-sterile plants can be reproduced vegetatively by divisions or cuttings, but they won't produce viable seed unless there's another plant in the vicinity that isn't a division of the same clump. In other words, dog-fennel is safe to grow, provided that all the plants grown are clones or genetically exact duplicates of one another. It is possible, therefore, to have this plant and enjoy its beauties without experiencing its brutal spread, provided that every plant is vegetatively propagated from the same stock. There is a risk, however. If I grow dog-fennel and a neighbor also grows it, and our plants have the slight genetic differences necessary for viable seeds to develop, there will be a population explosion. I certainly would not want to put this eupatorium in my garden if I lived in Chincoteague or anywhere else where there was a well-established local population of it, which rules out most of the Southeast. In my own garden I think I'm safe, however. The plant is not easily mistaken for anything else, and I've never noticed it growing anywhere in my county.

Joe Pye weed's transformation when moved from the wild into the garden is almost trifling compared with the metamorphosis dog-fennel undergoes—and in a garden of modest dimension it must be carefully sited. I grow it as part of a dense tangle of monumental plants used as a screen for privacy from our busy street. During a rapid spurt of growth in early summer, it towers to ten, even twelve feet. When it starts blooming in October it looks from afar like a great eruption of purple-tan smoke. Up close, it is breathtaking for its combination of large beauties with much tinier ones. The plant is very bold, rising from its base with stems growing very tightly together in their lower reaches. As they ascend, they spread outward, then weep downward. The little light pink flowers and the dark leaves are as finely detailed as the plumage of the snowy egret. The light plays on this plant and through it, and, as it is constantly moving, it fairly sparkles in bright sunlight. Furthermore, dog-fennel is so delicate that it does not block other beauties from view. It is another useful scrim plant which, despite its considerable height, can go near the front of a border. I look up, and through its tracery I see the clear bright azure of a late October afternoon sky. I lower my gaze, and through it I see the bright golds of perennial sunflowers, the pale blue of the tatar aster, the cranberry-toned foliage of Ravenna grass, the pewter fruits of bayberries.

It is a lovely thing, dog-fennel. But it still worries me just a little, and if I ever find a seedling, despite the reassuring words about its self-sterility, I will oust it in no time flat.

HELENIUM

I recently changed my mind about another North American native perennial—*Helenium autumnale*, or sneezeweed. After reading many years ago that several cultivars of helenium were useful as "bridge plants" (plants to tide us over between the end of the daylily season and the start of the autumn tide of chrysanthemums), I tried two, 'Bruno' and 'Butterpat', as I recall. They were so tall and gangly, and their colors were so muddy, that I composted them in their third year with little regret. Now I'm growing heleniums

Helenium 'Moorheim Beauty' holds center stage, with achilleas, *Artemisia lactiflora*, and echinops in the supporting cast in an Oregon garden.

again, but it's they who have changed, not me. Very imposing indeed is 'Gartensonne'—almost five feet tall, with bright golden flowers in late summer and early fall. But two new heleniums in particular strike me as likely to become indispensable. 'Feuersiegel' is a pinwheel of deep yellow splashed with scarlet, and 'Kugelsonne' is a remarkably clear primrose yellow. I grow these close to one another interspersed with *Artemisia* 'Valerie Finnis' and fountain grass. The cool silvery swags of the artemisia's flower stalks and the airy plumes of the grass's seed stalks are lovely in combination with the stronger colors of the heleniums.

The names of these heleniums are tip-offs that, once again, the Germans have been working on our native daisies. These European cultivars range in color from pale yellow to deep gold to russet. The blooming season is staggered, so that one or more will be in flower from mid-August until late October. Some are stiff and erect, others more spreading in habit. Considering that three or four of these cultivars are already on the market in America, and that the interplay between German and American nurseries is brisk of late, it seems inevitable that we will see much more of these really splendid new plants, and that they will become staples of the late border.

HELIANTHUS

If there's any one plant that suddenly awakened me to the rich but much-neglected possibilities of the garden in autumn, it was *Helianthus angustifolius.* Of all fall-blooming perennials, I prize most highly this sunflower. Although its native habitat is the wet lowlands of the eastern United States, it thrives in my well-drained sandy soil with only a slow, deep watering once a week. Even if it did not bloom at all, this helianthus would be worth growing for its foliage. (It does not in fact usually bloom in Great Britain, but it is grown there, precisely for its foliage.) Its narrow leaves are hairy to the touch, but they are so black a green that they seem lustrous from a few feet away. In habit, the plant looks something like an oleander.

This perennial sunflower is very tall. Some people chop it back

'Feuersiegel' (left) and 'Zimbelstern' (right) are just two of many hybrids of our *Helenium autumnale* and other North American species, bred in Germany and now beginning to take their proper place in American gardens.

Helianthus angustifolius, a very late bloomer that may not bloom at all north of New York City, is one of the final glories of the gardening year. In my New Jersey garden it blooms for three weeks starting around October 20.

halfway in late June to keep it under five feet, but I let mine assume its natural height of ten feet or more. It opens its blooms all up and down the plant more or less simultaneously, so that the effect is a sudden geyser of deep, rich gold. The single composite flowers catch the slanting light of autumn, also golden, in such a way as to quicken the pulse. Just one plant in a far corner lights up an entire garden with its radiance for three weeks at least. But this helianthus is very late as well as very tall. It starts blooming in the middle of October or even later, which means that people who live much farther north than New Jersey may seldom, if ever, have it in flower. It is winter hardy to −20 at least, but that isn't the point. It's the date of the first killing frost that determines whether the plant blooms.

There's a trick for success with this spectacular plant. It can't be stuck somewhere and then left to its own devices. For it to strut its stuff, it is crucial that clumps be lifted in early spring. Mere sprigs of new growth must be replanted, and the centers of the clumps thrown away. It also likes a new location each year. I learned this trick the hard way the second year I grew this sunflower, when I left it in place but gave a neighbor three tiny outside shoots. My helianthus was paltry that October, producing a slender crop of ho-hum little flowers. In my neighbor's garden, however, the new plants reached over thirteen feet. The shower of gold was so dazzling that I thought Zeus was back and up to some old tricks. Now I guarantee one of the best shows of late autumn by taking the time in spring to treat *H. angustifolius* to a new patch of earth.

LESPEDEZA

The first time *Lespedeza thunbergii* 'Albiflora' bloomed for me, it brought a great surprise. One of my neighbors thought the description of this Japanese bush clover in the Wayside Gardens catalogue made it sound like just what he needed for a place in front of his pond—a tall, late-blooming froth of pure white flowers. He ordered his from Wayside. I got mine from Holbrook Farm. We both received good plants in early May that lost no time in bursting into vigorous growth. In August, we started looking for buds, but new leaves just kept appearing until our plants stood some four feet high, a symmetrical fountain of growth. Even if it didn't flower, this lespedeza would be worthwhile for its striking form. It looks like a shrub, though it's actually a herbaceous perennial.

My neighbor's lespedeza beat mine by a few days, finally bursting into abundant and dramatic bloom on September 15, producing great clusters or sprays of tiny pealike flowers, pristine and glistening white. A few days later, when it started blooming, I discovered that mine was a lespedeza with a difference. There were sprays of glistening white, yes. But others—on the same plant—were deep rose. Still others were candy-striped, white, and several different shades of pink. I was puzzled, but a week or so after my particolored lespedeza came into bloom, a letter arrived from Allen Bush,

Physostegia 'Vivid', the rose-purple form of *Lespedeza thunbergii* and *Boltonia* 'Pink Beauty', weave together in a harmony that is no less beautiful for being subtle and muted.

sent to all of his customers who had bought it from Holbrook Farm that spring. Here's part of it:

> Oops. We may have been the victims of the unstable nature of one of our plants.
>
> In the past few weeks we watched in bewilderment: our crop of *Lespedeza* 'Albiflora' came into flower and a full third of these were variously colored pink or bicolor (pink and white).
>
> We facetiously wondered if anabolic steroids may have played a hand in this mystery, but after a few calls to some good gardening buddies we found out that the plant does take the occasional notion to turn colors other than pure white.
>
> So with egg on my face, I am writing to check and see how yours did this year. If your *Lespedeza thunbergii* 'Albiflora' didn't behave as expected, please let us know and we'll make amends with a refund or credit toward a future purchase.

I'd never gotten a plant recall notice before. But I ignored the offer of a refund or a credit, being perfectly content with this fickle lespedeza. Now, however, I've enlarged my collection to include *L. thunbergii* 'Albiflora' in its true white form as well as plain old *L. thunbergii*, which has magenta flowers. Another species, *L. japonica*, bears pure white flowers on gracefully arching stems. Planted with salvia 'Indigo Spires', it is a splendid sight in late September when the salvia's spikes and the lespedeza's trusses of flowers dance in the wind.

LIRIOPE

Many local nurseries sell the common kind of lilyturf or liriope (*Liriope muscari*), but for the most part it is a "pass-along plant," one that goes from one neighbor to another up and down the block or across the alley. I got one clump of it in this way about ten years back, and now, after dividing the plants repeatedly, I have great

sheets of it as ground cover. Liriope has high merit. It requires no maintenance beyond an annual shearing in late winter before the new leaves appear. It is evergreen, and its growth is so dense that weeds don't have a chance to penetrate it. Its tubers, like those of asparagus ferns, store water sufficiently to make it drought-proof. Its stiff spikes of flowers in September are a pleasant shade of light violet, and they last for weeks. *Liriope muscari* may not produce fruits in the colder areas of the country and may not in fact even survive in the very coldest parts, where *L. spicata,* a much more rugged species, may be substituted. But in my garden, the tiny flowers are followed by a fat crop of conspicuous berries. Dark jade green in early October, they turn black as they ripen. Some of them always persist through the winter, a pretty sight.

As ground cover or an edging, liriope has another benefit, as measured against some other plants used in similar ways. It bears no vigorous and invasive rhizomes or stolons to help it spread insidiously beyond its assigned territory. It is a well-behaved plant, almost content to do only what a gardener asks of it. (I say "almost

Liriope 'Silvery Sunproof' and *Verbena canadensis* grow peacefully together, neither trying to muscle the other aside, so long as the liriope is planted in clumps rather than in a continuous sheet.

content" because its fruits can and do germinate to produce new plants in unwanted locations. They are, however, easy to identify, and they are slow starters that can be pulled up with little trouble.) Liriope, incidentally, is usually listed as a plant for shade. It does well in shade or partial shade, but in my garden it grows equally well in full sun. In the South, however, it may appreciate the protection of at least light shade.

But there are other liriopes besides the pass-along kind, and they are of greater moment. 'Gold Banded', 'John Burch', and 'Variegata' all have lilac or lavender flowers, plus variegated green-and-gold foliage. 'Silvery Midget' and 'Silvery Sunproof' add the silvery touch their names imply. 'Royal Purple' has unusually impressive spikes of bloom. The color is very saturated and intense, and its bloom extends into late October, as does that of 'Munroe's White', whose individual blossoms look like baby pearls. Ordinary *L. muscari* is a workhorse of a plant, admirable for the service it renders. Plain truth and straightforward speaking demand that it be called attractive, but not breathtaking. These newer liriopes developed in cultivation are interesting in and of themselves. A few clumps planted amidst small ferns, rather than as a ground cover or an edging, more than hold their own.

LOBELIAS

Two of the best native perennials of early autumn are lobelias—*Lobelia cardinalis* and *L. siphilitica*. Both will bloom well in either full sun or partial shade, but they insist on moist soil. I grow them at the edge of a little artificial bog we made in our sandy soil some years ago by excavating a pit, lining it with a large sheet of butyl rubber, burying a rubber soaker hose at the bottom, and then returning the soil to the hole. I can't think of another flower as deeply saturated a dark red as *L. cardinalis*, which has a sheen like silken velvet. It is well worth the effort to seek out the forms that have dark red-brown leaves and beet-red stems, as these add to the play of deliciously sullen color. *L. siphilitica*, whose species name refers to its former use in medicine to treat venereal disease, has fine and vibrant green foliage. It starts blooming late in August,

In my garden a pot of a dwarf geranium named 'Smarty' ended up by pure accident next to a clump of *Liriope* 'Munroe's White', to serendipitous outcome.

with long-lasting deep blue flowers on tall stems that keep getting taller as the flowering season progresses and that finally arch forward under their own weight. It can take either full sun or partial shade, but it does best in slightly moist soils. It combines very well indeed with the tall white Japanese anemone 'Honorine Jobert'. We-Du offers a white form of this lobelia, as well as the more common blue. There are two hybrids between *L. cardinalis* and *L. siphilitica*. *L. x gerardii* bears deep purple flowers for almost two months. 'Rose Beacon' is an intense deep pink. Both plants are splendid and enlarge the color range of the genus.

In the cool light of the Pacific Northwest, the sullen-hued spikes of *Lobelia splendens* (left) appear more intense than ever. Our native *L. siphilitica* (right) deserves a better Latin name than the startling one it got, to indicate its former medical uses, for it possesses quiet grace and charm.

Although its seeds were collected in South Korea only in the mid-1980s, all who have grown or seen *Patrinia scabiosifolia* agree that it is one of the finest plants of autumn, with a great future before it.

PATRINIA

About one Asian perennial with an exciting future in the late summer and fall garden, there is some confusion. It is *Patrinia scabiosifolia.* The few reference books on my library shelves that list it offer it no praise, say that it is native to Japan, and claim that it is a summer bloomer. Here is an instance where genus and species names just aren't enough to distinguish an individual plant. One *P. scabiosifolia* is in fact a Japanese native, blooms in the summer, and may not be worth growing, though I haven't personal experience sufficient to make an informed judgment. The other form of *P. scabiosifolia,* however, is native to Korea, where seeds were collected in 1984 by Barry Yinger, who led the National Arboretum's plant-collecting expedition there that year. The Korean form blooms much later than the Japanese kind, whose seeds are currently the ones in American seed catalogues. But seed distribution from the Arboretum's program has worked so successfully that a few perennial nurseries are beginning to offer the Korean plants. More will surely follow, for to see this patrinia in the fall is to know the true meaning of lust. We-Du and Montrose, once again, are good sources.

This Korean patrinia, which grows about four feet high, blooms in August, but the flowers are not the thing. After the petals fall off, the seed pods turn bright yellow as they ripen, giving the plant the look of a yellow Queen Anne's lace. At the same time, the stems change to a luscious orange, and the leaves take on a bronzish purple tint. The seed heads and stems can be dried and keep enough of their spectacular color to make them prized additions to winter arrangements.

POKE

A friend in Massachusetts startled me by proclaiming it to be among the world's most beautiful of plants, especially during the autumn. She mentioned suddenly seeing on a September morning something as gleaming as rubies and garnets in a far corner of her garden, walking down to investigate, and then feeling shock when she saw what it was. What it was, was pokeweed *(Phytolacca americana).*

And indeed, to the unprejudiced eye (and the uninformed mind) our native pokeweed is a fetching plant, from the first emergence of its succulent and edible shoots in the spring. In summer its leaves remain fresh and green, even in drought. By late summer, it assumes a lovely, widely spreading habit and begins to produce graceful long clusters of white flowers.

But poke (the word is American Indian in origin) does not reach its true excellence until fall. Then the stems become a glowing, somewhat translucent shade of cranberry red with purple overtones. After the shiny jade berries deepen to black-purple, they attract many birds. Over fifty different kinds, including doves and cedar waxwings, devour the berries with huge enjoyment, sometimes becoming drunk on them.

Pokeweed delighted Henry David Thoreau, who wrote in "Autumnal Tints," one of his last essays, "Its cylindrical racemes of berries of various hues, from green to dark purple, 6 or 7 inches long, are gracefully drooping on all sides, offering repasts to the birds, and even the sepals from which the birds have picked the berries are a brilliant lake-red, with crimson, flame-like reflections, equal to anything of the kind—all on fire with ripeness." He also, I believe, used one of its long stems as a makeshift walking stick.

Some British gardeners, such as Beth Chatto, have paid high praise to poke, and a leading German seed company offers it. But it has two demerits. First, it's the very model of a successful weed. Those fifty kinds of birds that relish its fruits excrete its seeds wherever they fly, a large territory. Pokeweed couldn't do a better job of reproducing itself if it sprouted its own wings. The seeds, furthermore, are viable for years, exceeding the usual life span of humans. If buried by cultivation, they can lie dormant for as long as a century. If the soil is then disturbed and they are brought near the surface, they will germinate.

The house I live in was built around 1812. I'm always disturbing the surface of the soil around it, and always discovering new poke seedlings every spring. The thought that they may have grown from seeds a waxwing excreted when my great-grandparents were still in their cribs gives me a sense that I'm linked with history. It also suggests that pokeweed and I will go on forever—or that it will go on forever, and I will dig it up the rest of my days as a gardener.

Poke's second demerit is that it's poisonous, although as I've said already, gardens would be duller places if all toxic plants were eliminated. The young greens are edible, as what Southerners call "poke sallit"—"sallit" in the Elizabethan English meaning of cooked greens. They are toxic enough, however, that they should be cooked for a long time, with two changes of water. The berries are also poisonous, though not nearly as poisonous as the roots, which contain the dangerous alkaloid phytolaccatoxin.

I weed out poke every spring, but usually there's one plant somewhere that I miss, which makes itself known to me by suddenly being five feet tall. I let it be until the berries are fully ripe. It is another one of those harmonious connections between my garden and the natural landscape. When it is "all on fire with ripeness," poke is one of the most beautiful tokens of an American autumn.

SALVIAS—ONE MORE TIME

Many salvias are long-blooming annual or perennial lingerers, as was discussed in the previous chapter, but other salvias, some of the loveliest, are true plants of autumn. One is our native *Salvia azurea* 'Grandiflora' (listed by some nurseries as *S. pitcheri*), which starts blooming in late August and keeps on past frost. Its flowers are precisely what its specific name claims, the blue of the sky on a clear fair day. It will grow five feet tall, but if it isn't staked, the stems will end up on the ground. The color makes this chore entirely worthwhile. Another fine native species is *S. leucantha*. It is a perennial, but a tender one. It will scorch badly in a light freeze, and it isn't root hardy much below 25 degrees. But it's still a wonderful plant, worth the trouble of ordering every spring from one of the mail-order nurseries that carry it. A small rooted cutting will quickly put on size, becoming almost shrublike, around four feet tall and as wide, with narrow and pointed olive-green leaves

with gray on their undersides. In mid-September the first spikes of buds appear. They at first have an odd droop that calls to mind the gooseneck lysimachia *(Lysimachia clethroides),* but by early October they have straightened out, making a quiet kind of splash in their corner of the garden. The stem, where the first flowers appear, changes from green to royal purple. On some, the flowers are lilac; on others, white. Both have a purple and very velvety calyx, as pleasing to the touch as it is to the eye. Then there's another salvia I know less about than I would like. It may be a hybrid. It blooms so late that it's risky where frosts come early, because it is very sensitive to cold. It passes among my circle of gardening friends under the simple name of 'Late Blue Giant'. The foliage is Oz green, and the hyacinthlike spikes of large flowers are as blue as sapphires.

I am also much taken with 'Purple Majesty', a hybrid between *S. guaranitica* and *S. gesneriflora.* This September and October bloomer grows three feet high and spreads as wide. The dark and shining leaves set off nicely the abundant deep purple blossoms on long stems. It looks splendid growing with 'Belize', a selected form

Mexican sage *(Salvia leucantha)* (left) blooms very late, and except in the Deep South should be treated as an annual. It is nonetheless worth the trouble. Equally tender *Salvia vanhouttei* (center) is little grown at present. Its exuberant bloom, in an unusual garnet red, recommends it very highly. *Salvia azurea* 'Grandiflora' (right) is winter hardy, but it sprawls and must be staked. Stake it I do; no other flower has so celestial a blue.

of a species from Costa Rica with maroon-tinged somber green foliage and smoldering dark red blooms. I am also much impressed with *S. vanhouttei,* which makes a spreading plant two feet high and two feet across, and which is extremely generous in its crop of spikes of garnet flowers. Finally, among the late salvias are the various hybrids of our native *S. greggii.* Sandy Mush Herb Nursery offers several cultivars, including 'Furman's Red', 'Maraschino', 'Plum Wine', and 'Raspberry Royale'. The latter three are pastel shades of pink and light purple and occasionally will survive the winter in Zone 7.

SEDUMS

I can't think of more useful garden plants than the huge number of species and cultivars of sedums. The genus is a large one, with at least six hundred species native to the temperate zones, and there is an enormous range of variation among these amiable succulents. Some are fairly large, others are tiny. Some are reliably hardy in very cold regions, others are not. Some go dormant in winter, some in summer, and some are evergreen. The foliage ranges from emerald green to gray to blue-gray to reddish purple to almost chocolate brown, and there are variegated sorts as well. The clusters of flowers may be small and reticent or large and prominent. Provided that they grow in a climate suitable for the kind they need little attention. A few, like the golden-moss sedum or *Sedum acre,* will quickly cover a huge territory, but not in a menacing way, since this low ground cover grows around other plants rather than smothering them.

Sedums also vary so much in their season of bloom that some sedum or other will be in flower except in winter. But the finest sedums of all in my view are those that bloom in the autumn. The starting point, of course, is sedum 'Autumn Joy'. Is there any gardener left who hasn't heard of it by now? Hybridized in Germany, probably as a cross between *S. spectabile* and *S. telephium,* and introduced there as 'Herbstfreude', it made its way to England, where it was rebaptized with an exact translation of its German name. From England, it crossed the Atlantic to enliven our gardens

with the many dramatic changes it undergoes from summer right into winter. This sedum has attractive, fleshy, gray-green leaves from its first appearance in early spring, when it may be easily rooted from cuttings. In midsummer, the flattened, pale green, broccolilike clusters of flower buds appear. In late August, astonishing numbers of bumblebees, honeybees, wasps, and flies congregate on the blossoms as they open. (They do not necessarily drink the nectar, but seem at times to be lolling in stupefaction, like punks on a street corner.) The blossoms are creamy ivory at first, but there's a succession of colors that moves to pink, deep cherry-rose, russet, copper, and finally the dark mahogany of the seed heads, which remain handsome in winter, especially against a contrasting background of fresh-fallen snow. And if snow falls on

In high autumn, many ornamental grasses change to parchment-tan, *Sedum* 'Autumn Joy' undergoes the last of its myriad color changes before its seed heads darken to mahogany, and Japanese maples are in their final flame.

Sedum 'Vera Jameson' (left)
forms a low mound in October if
it is sheared back in late June.
Sedum sieboldii (right) is elegant
even in late September, before its
flowers appear, for its steely foliage and arching stems. Opposite:
In a border at the New York Botanical Garden, *Sedum* 'Autumn
Joy' takes its final bow. Behind it
are the white daisy flowers of *Asteromoea mongolica*. Behind them
wave the flower plumes of *Miscanthus sinensis* 'Zebrinus'.

a still day, it accumulates on the seed heads in little rounded
mounds, like igloos.

The spectacle 'Autumn Joy' stages begins early and unfolds
over several months. Other sedums put on a display that is no less
charming for being later and briefer. One such is *Sedum* 'Vera
Jameson,' a small plant that bears pink blossoms above deep pur-
ple-brown leaves and stems. One of its parents (the other may be
'Ruby Glow', though there's some uncertainty here) is *S. maximum*
'Atropurpureum', a rather lanky species with sprawling tendencies,
but remarkable for its purple leaves. Another, much smaller
sedum, is *S. brevifolium,* which begins to get interesting late in
August, when its small gray rosettes send up diminutive gray
towers of bloom stalks. The buds stay tight for weeks, then in
mid-October open into tiny cream flowers, with orange stamens so
prominent that they give the plant a whiskered look.

Finally, in late October, comes my last and my favorite sedum
of all. It is *S. sieboldii,* which forms a mound of arching stems
bearing succulent grayish blue leaves. The clusters of lavender-
pink blossoms announce that the end of another autumn is soon at
hand, but they do so with a benediction, not an elegy.

SOLIDAGO AND SOLIDASTER

If a horticultural Kingdom of God ever arrives in America, I think I know what its first sign will be: gardeners, more of us anyway, will start planting solidagos. Sensible and wise gardeners in Europe and Great Britain have planted them for over a century, and with great pride in the result. William Robinson was crotchety about them, of course, but then he was crotchety about many a matter. Solidagos, he wrote in *The English Flower Garden* (fifteenth edition, 1934) "exterminate valuable plants and give a coarse aspect to the border. They are also gross feeders and impoverish the soil." But other British writers, including Gertrude Jekyll, have had much kinder things to say about the genus.

The reason that Americans don't plant solidagos is that their common name is goldenrod, and we think we know all about goldenrods. Goldenrod, someone in our family will have told us when we were children, causes hay fever, allergies, watering eyes, and itching noses, visits to doctors, medications that make us drowsy, and similar evils in late summer and autumn. Bees and butterflies know better. They are great habitués of goldenrods, whose nectar they seek avidly. The plants that are the culprits in hay fever spread their tiny grains of pollen on the wind, and so don't need to produce nectar to attract insects to aid them in achieving their reproductive agenda. Goldenrods are innocent, and our wariness of them unjustified.

But there's more involved here, I think, than mistaken notions about what causes hay fever. Those British and European horticulturists who are keen on solidagos see them for the most part as exciting New World plants. Only one species, *Solidago virgaurea*, is native to Europe, and this fact means that Europeans can appreciate the great wealth of native North American goldenrods that we so casually overlook.

I happen to think that a garden is as suitable a home for goldenrods as is a roadside or a meadow or a marsh, but I also strongly advise that anyone who shares my view refrain from driving out into the countryside with a shovel in the trunk to collect a few. For one thing, despite the seemingly overabundant supply

of solidagos in the wild, one species native to North Carolina, *S. porteri,* hasn't been seen since 1899 and is believed to be extinct. Two others, the Houghton goldenrod *(S. houghtonii)* of New York and the Blue Ridge goldenrod *(S. spithamaea),* are either endangered species or close to it. Rather than collect a goldenrod (or any other wildflower, for that matter) and thereby contribute to its loss in the wild, it is far better to buy plants from nurseries that grow their own plants from seed. And even here, a bit of caution is in order. Some of the goldenrods grown and sold commercially, such as *S. microcephala,* will spread by underground stems at breakneck speed, bent on turning a varied garden into a colony of their particular species. *S. graminifolia* is a pretty little thing, but a tiny plant will within a year cover far too much territory. It also is subject to a disfiguring rust disease almost impossible to eliminate.

Gardeners in Europe and Britain have long valued the goldenrod, a New World plant that Americans tend to view as a wilding that should be left to roadsides. This English border is testimony to the goldenrod's rightful place in the garden.

Among the other species, *S. altissima* is fine. It spreads some-what by stolons, but it lacks real viciousness. *S. rugosa* is good too. It produces a few stolons, but for the most part it stays in a clump. Its one-sided panicles of golden flowers on stems four feet tall give it a graceful weeping look. Few could fault the seaside goldenrod, *S. sempervirens,* a clump-former with shining foliage (evergreen in the South) that bears wandlike sprays of good, clear yellow flowers. Growing up to 7 ½ feet in fertile soil, the red stems of the seaside goldenrod tend to drape over other plants in pleasant combinations, and they move beautifully in the slightest breeze. The fourth member of this quartet of native goldenrods is the sweet goldenrod, *S. odora,* another clump-former and distinctive for the pleasing anise scent of its leaves. Steeped in boiling water for half an hour, at a ratio of a cup of leaves to two cups of water, and strained and returned to boil for three or four minutes with ⅓ cup sugar and a tablespoon of pectin, this plant produces a delicious jelly. It also is historically significant. In 1773, when American colonists dumped the tea imported from England into Boston Harbor, they switched to "liberty tea" made from the leaves of *S. odora.*

There are, it is worth mentioning, a number of hybrid cultivars of solidago that were bred in Great Britain earlier in our century, including 'Golden Mosa', 'Cloth of Gold', and 'Peter Pan'. I have grown 'Peter Pan' with good luck, but it blooms in midsummer, not fall, and friends in the South have given up on it because it is subject to several diseases. A related hybrid curiosity is *x Solidaster luteus,* which brings to mind the common association of asters and goldenrods along American roadsides and in our fields. In the solidaster these two genera of wildflowers combine in quite a different way, for it is a bigeneric hybrid, a cross made in Lyon, France, in 1910 between an American aster, *Aster ptarmicoides,* and a goldenrod whose exact species is not known. (Similar bigen-eric crosses have been made in Great Britain, sometimes called *x Solidaster,* sometimes *x Asterago.*) From a distance, *x Solidaster* looks like a little lemon-yellow goldenrod, but with an airy and spreading flower panicle. Up close, however, the individual florets show off the aster part of their heritage, appearing as tiny daisies. The offspring of an odd marriage between two of America's most

The long-lasting flowers of *x Solidaster luteus* (top and center) come from an odd arranged marriage between a goldenrod and an aster. The range of color between cream and light yellow is variable. Solidaster makes a wonderful cut flower. An unidentified species of solidago (bottom) grows at Mt. Auburn Cemetery, Cambridge, Massachusetts, near the grave of Mary Baker Eddy.

noble native plants, the solidaster is also remarkable for a prolonged season of bloom, as many as two months in a favorable year,
beginning in late summer. Because it is a very durable and long-
lasting cut flower, this plant is now being widely raised under glass
in the Netherlands for shipment to florists in the United States and
other countries.

TRICYRTIS

The tricyrtis, or Japanese toad lily, takes some getting used to.
The adjective that seems to be most common in describing the
plant's flowers is "weird"; they look almost as though they evolved
on some other planet. I don't know what toads have to do with
them—or they with toads—but if I believed in visiting extraterres-
trials, I'd be willing to believe that tricyrtises were one of their gifts
to our planet.

I got started with toad lilies a few years back with the most
common species in the mail-order nursery trade, *Tricyrtis hirta.* By
the middle of its first October, it had formed a substantial clump
of some ten stems, each growing to about three feet high, with a
gracefully arching habit. Even during the summer, months before
it bloomed, the long and pointed, slightly hairy deep green leaves
gave the plant an appealing texture. One thing is clear about this
species and other plants in the genus: they need a location where
they can be seen up close, so as to allow them to be appreciated
in all their complexity. At the end of each stalk, there is a much-
branched cluster of ten or more flowers. The flowers, which balloon
before opening, like platycodons and fuchsias, have six petals, each
reflexed upward. Their background color is pink, but they are
heavily leopard-spotted with dark maroon and speckled with white.
Rising above the petals from the cup of the bloom, a thick style,
also gaudily spotted, lifts the flower's three pistils and six anthers.
Besides the flowers at the terminus of its stalk, *T. hirta* bears other
flowers, individually or in twos or threes, in the leaf axils along the
stems. The stems are downy, and the dark plum-purple buds are
ringed at their bottoms by odd little spurlike protuberances.

Other tricyrtis soon joined *T. hirta* in a moist spot at the front

of one border shaded by a dawn redwood and a tall viburnum. 'White Towers' bears pure white flowers, sans spots, on stems that arch even more than those of *T. hirta. T. formosana* echoes the pink and purple tones of *T. hirta,* but it grows a foot taller and is upright rather than arching. It produces a veritable candelabrum of bloom. Somewhat lower, at about two feet tall, *T. x* 'Sinonome' displays vivid purple spots against a contrasting background of sparkling white. It is stoloniferous, spreading in the course of two or three years into an impressive colony. As for other of my tricyrtis, I cannot say exactly what they are. Like aquilegias and hellebores, the species and cultivars in this genus hybridize so easily among one another that every year brings the fun of new surprises in their progeny.

Tricyrtis formosana, one of several species of Japanese toad lilies, has an odd beauty that takes time to appreciate but ultimately proves bewitching. Its strangely spotted and peculiarly constructed flowers appear on gracefully arching stems.

Bulbs of Autumn

When we think of autumn and of bulbs, we usually leap to thoughts of trowels and tulips, to fall planting of the great multitude of bulbs that will bloom the following spring, from the first crocuses of early March to the last sweet-smelling jonquils of late May. But autumn also has its own bulbs, using the word loosely to include corms, rhizomes, and tubers as well as bulbs in the strict botanical sense.

Autumn bulbs don't compare in number to the bulbs of spring or even those of summer, and some are rare to the point of being unavailable through commercial channels. I have in my own garden, for example, a fall-blooming snowflake *(Leucojum autumnale)* and a fall-blooming pink scilla *(Scilla scilloides)* grown from seed collected in Korea in 1985, but they were gifts from friends, and

I have never seen either listed in a catalogue. Apart from the rarities, however, there are enough commonly available autumn bulbs to enliven the late-season garden with their good cheer and great charm.

ALLIUMS

The bulbs longest associated with the human race are those in the genus *Allium.* The onion was one of the very first vegetables to be domesticated, in prehistoric times. Leeks, shallots, garlic, and chives all assumed an early prominence in the world's cuisine (both high and low), a position they have steadfastly maintained. These are surely blessed plants.

Alliums have a place in the pleasure garden, as well as in the vegetable garden. One of their number, to be sure, is a curse to gardeners with lawn fetishes: the common wild onion is one of the nastiest of the perennial weeds of winter and spring. But the genus evens the balance with other species of high ornamental value, such as the Himalayan *Allium giganteum,* with its immense starburst of lilac-purple flowers topping stems rising between three and four

Garlic chive *(Allium tuberosum)* does double duty. Its flowers in September are fetching, and its wide and flattened leaves lend pungency to salads and meats.

feet tall in June. The silvery seed heads persist into fall. They are splendid for dried arrangements, but if left in the garden they will eventually fall off, blowing around like tumbleweed and scattering seeds that will sprout in unexpected places.

Many species of alliums have long finished blooming by midsummer, but fall has its species too, starting around Labor Day, when the garlic chive, or *Allium tuberosum,* begins to open its clusters of silvery white flowers. Garlic chives do double duty. The leaves are a tasty garnish for salads and soups, and when baked with chicken, lemon juice, and a bit of olive oil make a fine and easy main dish. The flowers, on stems that grow to about eighteen inches, are elegant and airy in mixed arrangements. If the flower stalks are removed promptly, the garlic chive will bloom a second time, in midautumn. But the plant comes with a caveat: gardeners who don't deadhead it before its seeds mature and scatter may soon find that they are growing far more garlic chives than they planned or cared to have.

Somewhat later blooming and less rambunctious than *A. tuberosum* are *A. senescens* 'Glaucum', which bears lavender-pink flowers above gray-blue foliage, and *A. stellatum,* whose blossoms are a fine, deep violet-pink. Rounding out the allium year in late October, *A. kurilense* stands out for its drooping heads of reddish lavender flowers.

CANNAS

America's long, if for the moment much cooled, love affair with the canna began in 1777 in southern Louisiana, when the Quaker botanist William Bartram first spotted the native species *Canna indica* growing in wetlands. In his *Travels Through North and South Carolina, Georgia, East and West Florida* (1792), he described the hardships of his journey of exploration—the clouds of biting mosquitos, the danger from alligators—but then went on to write glowingly about the cannas he found "in surprising abundance, presenting a gorgeous show; the stem rises six, seven, and nine feet tall, terminating upwards with spikes of scarlet flowers."

No plant was more characteristic of nineteenth-century garden-

Somewhat later blooming and less likely to spread itself far and wide than the garlic chive is *Allium senescens* var. glaucum.

ing than the canna. In both Great Britain and Europe, it was feverishly hybridized to produce new cultivars from species found in Central and South America and in the tropical Pacific. Like elephant ears, castor beans, and potted banana plants, it lent to gardens in the north temperate zone a look of the jungle and a touch of the exotic.

It is easy to understand our Victorian ancestors' affection for cannas. Their large leaves, ranging from deep green to brownish maroon, unfurl with dramatic boldness. Their immense flower trusses, in shades of pink or orange or red or yellow, put on a good show from late summer until frost. Each stalk, if cut back after the last pointed bud opens its last opulent blossom, will soon be replaced by a successor. Left to themselves, the flowers will be followed by appealingly bold and bristly seed pods.

Cannas are easy to grow and remarkably immune to disease, although snails and slugs can riddle them. In the Deep South, they go dormant in late autumn but successfully overwinter in the earth. In Zone 7 and farther north, they should be watered well just before the first hard freeze and then dug and dried for winter storage in dry sand in a cool basement or closet. They may be planted outdoors as soon as all danger of frost is past, but I delay planting until mid-June, thus putting off their peak of bloom until September.

I like cannas, but not everyone shares my view. They haven't been in vogue in years. They are old-fashioned plants, more likely to be found in dooryard gardens in the South than in suburban ones in the North. I suspect that they fell out of favor because the conventional way of planting them, at the center of round beds dotted meaninglessly about plots of green turf, was an ugly and persistent fashion. The best uses of cannas are not in these round beds, where they still are sometimes seen (especially in public parks). They are good background plants in a border. They are also good dot or accent plants, used in groups of three in a mixed bed. They are lovely in masses, particularly the pastel shades and those with purple or reddish foliage. (In one of the most beautiful gardens I know, the bulb garden high on the slopes of Montjuich in Barcelona, rivers of thousands of pale pink cannas flow down through

In a mixed border of perennials and ornamental grasses, the dramatically backlit foliage of cannas contributes an almost tropical note.

the landscape, a glorious sight in the lambent golden light of a late afternoon in October. Even true canna-haters—and there are some—would be converted as instantly as St. Paul on the road to Damascus.)

I suspect that cannas are about to have their day once again, and I'm glad. Older cultivars such as 'Red King Humbert' and 'President', raised in large quantities in Oklahoma, are easily available, but Georgia is now the center of the further development and improvement of the canna. There, hybridizers like Patrick Malcolm of TyTy Plantation have been busy for over a decade, raising thousands of seedlings and selecting the best for introduction. Among the newer cultivars are 'White Queen', 'Maudie Malcolm', and 'TyTy Red', all bred for a long season of bloom extending from sixty days after planting until frost, for huge flower trusses, and for hardiness to temperatures reaching zero. These new cannas vary considerably in height, lending themselves to many different uses. 'Omega' bears ugly, muddy-orange blossoms, but that doesn't matter; it grows so tall, up to sixteen feet by September in my garden, that the flowers can hardly be seen from the ground. It makes a dandy screen, and it sometimes fools visitors into thinking that I'm growing bananas in New Jersey. At the other extreme, 'Garbo', a salmon pink with red leaves, reaches only to eighteen inches. Other cultivars fall in between these two, with most of them standing between four and six feet tall.

COLCHICUM AND CROCUS

Nature often mimics herself, coming up with blossoms of similar appearance in plants that are not closely related. Thus it is with the cup-shaped flowers of colchicums and autumn crocuses. They closely resemble one another, but colchicums are members of the lily family, and crocuses are in the iris family.

I would not want to have a garden without a few colchicums at least. They always grew in my mother's garden in Texas, so they are part of my deepest memories. When my own family rented a farmhouse outside Clinton, New York, for three years in the mid-1960s, there were rows of ancient and immense clumps of a colchi-

When autumn's warm sunbeams strike them, the large chalices of *Colchicum autumnale* have an eerie glow that suggests the Holy Grail.

cum of unknown identity lining a path from the barn to an abandoned privy. The hundreds of large lavender flowers that sprang up each September were always startling but welcome, as they formed broad bands of fresh color against the green grass. The foliage, big floppy leaves that appeared in early spring and died back in early summer, was in its turn equally startling, seeming not at all to go with the flowers, in a disparity matching that of caterpillar and butterfly. In *A Prospect of Flowers* (1945), the British writer Andrew Young described the seasons of colchicum this way: "it gives a start of surprise to meet it in September; the leaves came in early summer, but they have withered away, the flowers appearing like a posthumous poem."

Two of America's classic garden writers were of different minds

Colchicums punctuate an array of plants with great autumn interest in a corner of the late Jane Pratt's fine garden in Portland, Oregon. From left are: the multitude of tiny, rusty-red fruits of an ornamental crab apple, the oddly clustered pink fruit of the beautyberry (*Callicarpa boninieri* var. giraldii), and *Aster* 'Harrington's Pink'.

about colchicums. Alice Morse Earle in *Old Time Gardens* (1901) didn't like the colchicum at all, feeling that it

> seems out of keeping with the autumnal season. Rising bare of leaves, it has but a seminatural aspect, as if it had been stuck in the ground like the leafless, stemless blooms of a child's posy bed. Its English name—Naked Boys—seems suited to it. The Colchicum is associated in my mind with the Indian Pipe and similar growths; it is curious, but it isn't pleasing.

Louise Beebe Wilder disagreed, writing in *Adventures with Hardy Bulbs* (1936) that

> Few flowers are more floriferous than Colchicums, and as this beauty is vouchsafed with the autumnal season, and they come blowing out of the earth with all the verve and enthusiasm that we associate with spring's manifestations, when most other plants are making their valedictory gestures, it is astonishing that they do not command more notice from gardening folk in general.

Crocus banaticus, native to the meadows of Yugoslavia and Romania, flowers in early October. A dozen or so bulbs of this or any other autumn crocus tucked into an odd corner provide an element of surprise.

I part company with Mrs. Earle in this matter and side with Mrs. Wilder. So also does Ann Lovejoy, who wrote to me late one September that

> My friend Daphne gave me a whole flat full of lavender, semi-double colchicums that she had thinned out of an overgrown bed in her old garden—we trade our garden weeds, for one person's bane may be another's treasure. We have swapped great bundles of her blue aconites for my white gooseneck loosetrife, canterbury bells for pink oenotheras, raspberries for rhubarb. These colchicums were especially welcome, for I want to put them beneath a small, elderly plum tree which carpets the grass with its fruit. The plums are rather wormy, but they look absolutely gorgeous when spangled with dew, their rich, plummy skin softened with a silvery bloom and faintly speckled with purple. I heaped straw mulch all around the tree, and when we till up the ground late in October, the colchicums will get tucked in to emerge next autumn amid the fallen fruit. Won't that look striking?

I believe that it will, and wish that I had my own elderly plum tree to borrow the effect.

My hero when it comes to planting colchicums, however, is Carl Krippendorf. In a letter to Elizabeth Lawrence, quoted in her little book, *Lob's Wood,* Mr. Krippendorf wrote from his country place near Cincinnati that he had counted seventy-seven flowers in one clump. "The flowers are coming up by the thousands," he continued. "They light up the woods when the sun is upon them. It almost seems that the light comes from within." In another letter to Miss Lawrence, he revealed a love for these bulbs that transgresses the line between enthusiasm and obsession. "I planted my first corms more than forty years ago, but I did not divide them for many years. If I had divided them regularly from the time they were planted I would have over fifty thousand now. What a lost opportunity. Today I counted between fifteen and sixteen thousand clumps, large and small."

I have neither the money nor the space to follow in Mr. Krippendorf's footsteps, but I do share his passion for colchicums. At the moment I am growing five kinds, four of which are in the lavender-purple to pink range of the spectrum. 'Lilac Wonder' and *C. bornmuelleri* are both splendid, and they have that inner radiance Mr. Krippendorf described. 'Waterlily', with large double pink flowers, is a wonderful sight. Just three or four bulbs make a grand display. 'Autumn Queen', which also goes about the world as 'Princess Astrid', is a pale purple, tessellated or checkered with a darker hue. As for *C. autumnale* 'Album', its enormous pure white chalices are breathtaking with black mondo grass (*Ophiopogon planiscapus* 'Nigresens') grown at their feet. Another ground cover that combines well with any of the colchicums is *Ceratostigma plumbaginoides*. Its azure fall blossoms nicely complement their lavender and lilac tones, and since it is one of the very latest perennials to emerge in the spring, very late in May, it will not be crushed by the ungainly colchicum leaves as they sprawl toward dormancy.

I can never turn the pages of *The Bulb Book* (1981) by Martyn Rix and Roger Phillips without a sigh when I get to the pages with handsome pictures of autumn crocuses. *Crocus boryi, C. laevigatus, C. vallicola*—the list goes on and on of toothsome-looking fall crocuses I will probably never get to grow because there are no commercial sources for them in North America. I must make do with only a few. One is *Crocus speciosus*, which ranges from blue-lavender toward light purple, with intricate stipples or stripes of a darker hue. The form I have looks blue at first glance or from a distance. A closer look shows it to be pale lavender, deepening in intensity along the edges of the petals and in the pronounced veins running from the center of the blossom, with fainter and very feathery subsidiary veins adding a more complex note. The prominent stamens are a strong apricot gold, and the shadows they cast on the petals in bright sunshine add an almost sculptural dimension to the bloom. The flowers have a delicate fragrance of lemon peel. The plant reproduces itself with gusto, both by forming a multitude of tiny cormlets, which can be dug up after bloom and spread around the garden, and by a generous crop of seeds. This crocus, the earliest of the season, has an ingratiating way of showing up in new spots, and the surprise is always a pleasant one. Its only fault is the frailty of its stems. It combines very well planted amongst a colony of yellow toadflax *(Linaria vulgaris)*, partly for support, partly for the good play of colors.

My second favorite common crocus is *C. sativus,* mostly purple, although again there is a color range. Its long golden styles protrude from the blossoms at odd angles, like lolling tongues. This particular crocus, of course, has enormous historical and economic importance, for from its roasted stigmas comes saffron, a spice that's worth its weight in gold. The plant was also the source of an important dyestuff in the ancient world. No other flower has as rich a history as the saffron crocus, which was held sacred both in ancient Egypt and in the Minoan civilization of Bronze-Age Crete. In centuries earlier than our own, it also was used as a drug to treat depression, jaundice, and the common hangover, among other maladies. (Despite the Egyptian connection, the rumor that "crocodile" means "a creature that dreads crocuses" is not supported by the nearest dictionary at hand, although I somehow wish that it were.) I have only a few bulbs of a variant form of the saffron crocus, *C. sativus* 'Cartwrightiana Albus', since they sell for $3 apiece, an effective price to discourage massed plantings.

My third crocus, which has only recently been available, through Wayside Gardens, is *C. goulimyi,* named for Dr. C. N. Goulimis, who discovered it in Greece in the mid-1950s. Edith Eddleman describes it as looking like little lavender-pink lollipops. I have borrowed from her the inspiration of planting it in the midst of a patch of *Verbena tenuisecta,* a pink form that harmonizes well with Dr. Goulimis's discovery. Like *C. speciosus,* this crocus multiplies prolifically. Its season of bloom is long, almost two months.

Finally, rounding out the autumn crocuses I have been able to obtain and grow, there are *C. medius,* a floriferous October bloomer, blue-purple with a crimson style, and *C. ochroleucus,* a soft white that blooms well into November. One Thanksgiving Day I saw it covered with a dusting of snow that vanished in early morning when the sun came out.

CROCOSMIAS

I see more and more evidence of these attractive hardy bulbs in the iris family in American nursery catalogues and gardens. Originating in the late nineteenth century at the Lemoine nursery in France, they were the results of hybridization between *Crocosmia aurea* and *C. pottsii,* both native to South Africa. Later breeding took place in Great Britain, some of it involving intergeneric crossing between another South African species, *C. masoniorum* and the closely related *Curtonus paniculatus.* The beauty of crocosmias when in flower lies in the brilliant colors of their blossoms, the elegant sweep of their oddly swerving spikes, and their emphatic leaves, which are much like those of the gladiolus. There is also high ornamental value in the sweeping seed stalks once their season of bloom has finished. Cultivars sold by some American nurseries include 'Emily McKenzie' (deep orange), 'Lady Wilson' (apricot), 'Norwich Canary' (glowing yellow), and 'Solfatare' (apricot gold). The one I like best is 'Lucifer', which produces a dramatic blaze of red-orange for several weeks starting in late August. Although descended from somewhat tender ancestors, the hybrid crocosmias are hardy at least to Zone 6, with a protective mulch of leaves. They do equally well in full sun or partial shade, but they seem better placed in a slightly shady location. Their hot colors are toned down there, and the note of warmth is welcome.

Crocosmias, considering their highly attractive foliage, their abundant bloom for over a month starting in mid-August, and their fine qualities as long-lasting cut flowers for mixed bouquets, are badly neglected by American gardeners at the moment. 'Lucifer', the one most commonly sold, can be difficult to site in a border. Its strong scarlet-orange calls for a careful choice in selecting its companions. I can't think of a better marriage than 'Lucifer' alongside the glowing blue-purple spikes of *Salvia guaranitica.*

CYCLAMENS

If I had to make do with just one kind of autumn-blooming bulb, it would be cyclamens. I do not mean the large and splashy hybrids of *Cyclamen persicum* that are raised in greenhouses and sold by florists during the winter. The cyclamens I have in mind are the much more diminutive and graceful wild species, some of which are perfectly hardy all over the United States. But praise for these cyclamen species must be tempered by a stern warning. Natives of the Mediterranean basin for the most part, they are endangered in the wild, thanks to unscrupulous collectors who sell them to the commercial bulb trade in Europe and the United States. Often they are mislabeled in such a way that an especially rare species may be identified as a more common one. Generally, if a tuber is gnarled and pocked it has probably been collected, for its scars are evidence of the rocky soil of the hillside where it originally grew. Buying these plants enriches their destroyers.

Fortunately, it is possible for American gardeners to grow hardy cyclamens with a clear conscience and the absolute knowledge that they are not helping bring about the plants' extinction in the wild. It is Nancy Goodwin who provides this clear conscience, and cyclamens as well. Some years ago, when she first saw some hardy cyclamens in England, she fell in love with them. Later, when she learned that collection from the wild put them in great danger, she got hold of seeds of as many species as she could find and began raising them. A small lean-to greenhouse followed, and then a much larger one at Montrose, the nursery she eventually founded in Hillsborough, North Carolina.

I got my first shipment of cyclamens from Montrose in September of 1986. Some, both pink and white forms of *C. hederifolium* (formerly *C. neapolitanum* and still listed under that name in some books), were already blooming in their pots, before their rather sharply pointed foliage appeared. Others, whose more rounded leaves identified them as several forms of *C. coum*, would not begin their season of bloom, which continues well into winter, until late fall. I planted the pots of *C. coum* immediately, but I delayed in planting *C. hederifolium*, placing the pots instead on a table on our deck so I could study the plants up close and at eye level. Everything about these tiny plants is a delight. The little, swept-back petals of the blossoms hover over the leaves like small butterflies. The foliage is as mottled as a trout, with markings of deep olive,

For a dry and shaded spot, hardy cyclamens are ideal. Here a pink form of *C. hederifolium* lifts its tiny and delicate blossoms in October.

metallic gray, and many shades of green. Each flower is borne individually on its own reddish brown stem, and in most species, as the petals drop once the blossom has been pollinated, the stem begins to coil, working its way back to the earth, where ants come later to carry off the seeds to other locations where they may germinate and grow.

More cyclamens have continued to come from Nancy Goodwin's nursery every autumn, and in 1988, on a crisp and sunny Saturday at the end of October, I finally went to the cyclamens at Montrose. They were everywhere, many thousands of them. Flats of nonhardy species such as *C. africanum* were brought outside during the day for pollination. The rock garden, the beds beneath the huge magnolia trees, the greenhouses—all were aglow with the

Later to bloom than *C. hederifolium*, *C. coum* produces its heart-shaped leaves before the flowers, in white or various shades of pink, begin to show.

delicate colors of cyclamens. In the woods, Nancy Goodwin has
more cyclamens than Carl Krippendorf had colchicums. They grow
in masses under the oaks and hickory trees, amidst emerald-green
moss. In some places on that fine October day, they were covered
by fallen leaves, so that I had to push the leaves aside to see the
troutlike foliage and butterfly flowers, and drop to my knees to take
a closer look at one of autumn's most beautiful plants, one that
makes up in elegance what it lacks in size. It was a moment marked
by a powerful sense of well-being and harmony with nature.

DAHLIAS

Dahlias, like cannas, are as much plants of late summer as of
autumn, and the first good frost also takes them out for the year.
I know gardeners for whom they are a consuming horticultural
passion, sometimes to the exclusion of all else, and passion in
gardeners is something I respect, even when the result is a back
garden composed entirely of row upon row of dahlias.

I have a strange tale about dahlias. My longtime friend George
Off was so widely respected and loved in horticultural circles here-
abouts that following his death in 1987, the Philadelphia Flower
Show was dedicated to his memory. George Off was known first and
foremost as an orchid man. His company, Waldor Orchids, in
Linwood, New Jersey, is a mecca for orchid lovers throughout the
Northeast, and Waldor has for many years been well known for the
spectacular displays it put on for the Philadelphia show. Water-
falls, tropical bird calls, even ferocious simulated storms with thun-
der and lightning and pattering rainfall that soon turned
torrential—any or all of these, as well as many thousands of orchids in full bloom, might be part of one of Off's dramatic displays

For years I've visited the Waldor greenhouses, near my house,
a couple of times a month. From time to time I pick up an orchid
or a tropical fern, but generally I just liked to chat with George Off
about plants. Waldor was open to the public until George Off died,
except for the very back greenhouse. And the very back greenhouse
had an exit with a sign warning that it was strictly forbidden to use.
I always respected the sign, though I was curious.

Even people who aren't keen on dahlias will find it hard to resist 'Japanese Bishop'. Its moderate stature, its clear scarlet, semidouble flowers, and its rich black-green leaves all make it work well with other plants in a herbaceous border.

The last autumn of George Off's life, I visited the greenhouse with a question I wanted to ask him. One of his sons said he was out back, working behind the greenhouse, and that I should just go on through the door—his father wouldn't mind. So I did, and there he was, tending to his dahlias. There were many rows of them, over a hundred plants, staked within an elaborate and permanent system of heavy metal pipes. The display of color—yellows of every hue, soft apricots, flamboyant oranges, deep maroons, crimsons and scarlets, almost every color except blue—was overwhelming. Some of the plants were ten feet high, and each one was firmly staked and properly disbudded to produce either the largest blossom possible or the greatest number of blossoms. George noticed my surprise. "I love orchids," he said, "but my true passion is dahlias, and my happiest gardening moments are those I spend here with them." I understood immediately. My friend was a closet dahliaphile, and I had learned his secret.

I went through a mild dahlia craze, myself, but that was many years back, and I finally got tired of all the staking and disbudding and tending they require. To hew an inch or two closer to the truth, I seldom got around to the work, and it was embarrassing to have friends visit my garden, see all the dahlias lying prone or leaning at strange angles with blossoms growing in peculiar directions. If a gardener is lazy and raises tall dahlias, the dahlias are great tattletales. I now grow only two dahlias. 'Park Princess' is a cactus type, deep pink; the plants grow only thirty inches high and don't need to be staked. 'Japanese Bishop'—a peculiar name, I think—has single, clear red flowers and leaves that are black above and pewter below. It looks stunning near berberis 'Rosy Glow'. Both of these dahlias make fine cut flowers for mixed fall arrangements. For the best fall bloom, planting in mid-June or even a week or so later is fine.

LYCORIS

It is habitual with gardeners to wish to grow plants they cannot succeed with because of where they live. People who live in New England would love to have gardenia hedges, if they could, and people in southern Alabama pine for peonies. As someone living in Zone 7, where *Lycoris radiata* or red spider lilies aren't reliably winter hardy, I envy my friends farther south for their good fortune in having them. These native Asian bulbs, which reached the United States in the early nineteenth century, quickly attained great popularity in our southern states. They are still widely planted there, and for good reason. The stems pop up in late August, bare of foliage, and almost overnight each stem is crowned with a ring of soft red flowers, made more graceful by the spidery pistils sticking out of the florets. In southern farmyard gardens, spider lilies are often seen planted in circular beds devoid of other vegetation. The effect is strange and magical, as if red fairy rings had suddenly appeared on the ground. Spider lilies don't drive away the torrid southern heat of very late summer, but they do bring a promise that it won't go on forever, that cool days will come soon.

There is one lycoris, *L. squamigera*, which is hardy farther north, well into Zone 5. It shares with the spider lily the habit of blooming in late summer or early fall, without foliage, but its blossoms are larger, and they are a deep lilac-pink, not red. It is pleasant enough, but I wish that *L. radiata* were the hardier one.

Grasses of Autumn

Ornamental grasses are splendid in autumn, but they really transcend any season. Calamagrostis, Ravenna grass, and many of the tall miscanthuses may be left standing all winter. Cut back in very early spring, when they will remain dormant until the first reliably warm days spur them into another season's growth, they are dramatis personae in a garden for almost ten months out of the year. A few of them, especially some of the carexes, retain their color for the whole twelve months. These grasses are thus to be accounted among the lingerers—and what lingerers they are!

It takes no keen power of observation to notice that grasses are enjoying enormous popularity in America nowadays. Although gardeners who wish to explore the full range of grasses and their best uses still must resort to the mail-order nurseries that specialize in them, many local garden centers and neighborhood nurseries now sell plastic tubs of the commoner forms of miscanthus and pennisetum. They are increasingly used in parks and public plantings, as well as in commercial landscaping of office buildings and even fast-food restaurants: three different kinds of miscanthus and several pennisetums conceal the bases of the golden arches of a Mc-Donald's a couple of towns up the road from my own house.

The reasons for the strong turn to ornamental grasses are several, and the first of them is ease. The words "no-maintenance gardening" are fool's gold, and most people know it. The only way to abolish maintenance is to remove everything that grows and replace it with asphalt or heavy plastic mulching film covered with small stones or gravel, and the result is not a garden. But reducing the amount of maintenance a garden requires is an understandable ambition, and one that these grasses go a long way to help achieve. All that my miscanthus and pennisetum ask of me is that I cut them back close to the ground once a year—an easy task that incidentally provides good material for mulching. (I have a friend who grows so many of these grasses that every March she makes a huge rounded pile of their dry foliage, stems, and seed tassels in a back corner of her garden to use as mulch later in the season. The pile itself is surprisingly attractive, reminiscent of those haystacks Monet painted in changing conditions of light.) The main thing to do with most of these grasses is to watch them grow and change with the seasons. Unlike lawn grass, they entail no burdensome and boring weekly chores, no noisy machinery to haul out of the shed and rev up, no waste of fossil fuel, and no pollution of the air. The larger grasses, furthermore, especially satisfy the impatient impulses that gardening often frustrates. They spurt into such rapid growth in the spring that the little blades of Ravenna grass *(Erianthus ravennae),* for example, which stick up only a few inches above the old clump on the first of May, will be shoulder high a month later. By the Fourth of July they may reach a stately twelve feet—or even taller, in fertile, moist soil. Other very tall grasses include the giant reed *(Arundo donax),* which looks a bit like corn on steroids and which can steeple up to twenty feet, and eulalia grass *(Miscan-*

thus sinensis), whose ambitions, if slightly less lofty, can still allow it to top off at almost ten feet. Only bamboo, itself a grass, grows at the furious pace of these giant grasses.

The prodigious heights of these particular grasses make them not especially well suited for small gardens, as they overwhelm everything else. They still have their uses, however. I will leave *A. donax* to others, but both Ravenna grass and eulalia serve me well. We live in a corner house on the busiest street in town, a favorite route for buses and trucks, as well as police cars, ambulances, and fire engines. The noise of traffic and the scream of sirens provide little tranquillity, and the foot traffic on our sidewalks is heavy during much of the year, since there is a school crossing at the corner. Just inside our front fence, before the tended part of the garden begins, I planted years ago a thicket of tall ornamental grasses, bayberries, and other native trees, and some tall pyracanthas. This tangled planting, in a band ten feet deep, gives us a visual barrier between the front garden and the constant traffic in the street, and it also muffles the noise.

Part of the appeal of ornamental grasses lies in their great diversity. Some may seem to wish to scale the heavens, defying the common conception of grass as something lowly and foot-trodden, but others hug the earth. *Holcus mollis* 'Variegatus', commonly known as variegated velvet grass for its green and white striped leaves with pinkish overtones, and for its downy texture, grows no more than six inches high. It spreads a bit, but *Festuca ovina* 'Glauca' forms little domes or mounds, also low to the ground at about eight inches. The tassels that form in June bring it to sixteen. *Carex morrowii* 'Variegata' forms not a mound but a mop, a busy little swirl of leaves that looks like some of Leonardo da Vinci's sketches of motion. Grasses of intermediate size include *Helictotrichon sempervirens*, which makes spiky clumps about three feet high, with leaves arching gracefully at their tips. There's also *Pennisetum alopecuroides* or fountain grass, which grows around 3 ½ to 4 feet tall and produces an abundance of feathery, pink-toned flowers in late summer. Fountain grass never overwhelms its neighbors in a border. I like to grow it around yuccas for the contrast between its subtle grace, delicate coloration, and yielding movement in even a

Broad sweeps of *Pennisetum alopecuroides* (foreground) and miscanthus hybrids lend a feeling of wildness and motion to a garden. The effect is heightened in autumn, when grasses are at their best, waving their flower and seed plumes above seas of tawny leaves that chatter in the wind.

slight breeze and the dark and sober green of the yuccas and their stiff and unmoving armament.

Among the miscanthus of less daunting scale than eulalia grass, there is the aptly named cultivar *Miscanthus sinensis* 'Gracillimus', which grows between four and six feet tall and makes a fine upright accent in a border. *Calamagrostis acutiflora* 'Stricta', with soft green leaves that weep slightly, forms a mound about the size of a bushel basket. In midsummer its narrow, erect, silvery-pink flower spikes rise like exclamation points to five feet. It combines pleasingly with *Artemisia lactiflora*, the ghostplant artemisia, the only species that's grown not for its foliage but for its flowers. In late July or early August *A. lactiflora* puts up a huge, open, and very feathery spike with hundreds of tiny light green buds. The spike rises some four feet, like an enormous astilbe. As its species name indicates, the buds of this artemisia turn milky white when they open. The panicle stays in bloom for at least two weeks, fading then to a beige seed plume that stays handsome throughout the autumn, as do the seed spikes of the adjacent clump of calamagrostis. The two plants make a happy marriage embracing both differences and similarities of form and texture.

Grasses also vary widely in their color, both in a single species over the span of a year and from one species to the next. The leaves of *Miscanthus sinensis,* a good shade of green in late spring and summer, gradually change to parchment tan as autumn wears on, and its pink flower tassels go through several transformations, changing to pale, pale gold, then to straw, and finally to light beige. Lyme grass *(Elymus canadensis),* a spreading and stoloniferous low plant that is tough enough to grow on coastal sand dunes, is a pale gray-blue. Bluer still are some of the fescues and blue oat grass *(Helictotrichon sempervirens). Pennisetum setaceum* 'Burgundy Giant' (unfortunately not winter hardy) has extremely handsome cordovan-purple leaves. *M. sinensis* 'Purpurascens' develops red tints in summer and by early October is almost scarlet. *Panicum virgatum* 'Rubrum', the red switch grass, shows reddish tones in the summer and turns crimson when nights begin to cool down. But the champion of all the red grasses is Japanese blood grass *(Im-*

The bad news about *Pennisetum setaceum* 'Burgundy Giant' (left) is that it will not survive cold winters. It is nonetheless so handsome for its purple foliage and graceful plumes that it is worth replanting each spring. *Miscanthus sinensis* 'Purpurascens' (right) blooms in summer, but its silvery seed heads remain attractive, especially when the leaves turn to their autumnal shade of red.

Blood grass (*Imperata cylindrica* 'Rubra'), especially when backlit by autumn's low-angle sunlight, blazes like fire. Here it is strikingly paired with *Alopecurus pratensis aureus* in Kurt Bluemel's garden in Maryland.

perata cylindrica 'Rubra'). Its leaves are dark burgundy for half their length at least from the time they first emerge in the spring. The color deepens in September and spreads to the entire length of the leaves. Backlit in the light of early morning or late afternoon, blood grass seems to be aflame. It is sensational when grown in combination with the silver-stemmed Russian sage *(Perovskia atriplicifolia)* and blue oat grass; in slanting golden light the plants radiate color and brilliance like fine old stained glass. I have also seen it used elegantly and unforgettably in the garden of the late Fred Meyer in Columbus, Ohio, planted in a row at intervals of about eighteen inches against the background of a pewter-gray succulent ground cover, *Orostachys furusei.* Grown with this companion, which forms a dense mat, blood grass resembles a little fountain of crimson-lighted water. Another of my favorite grasses—although in this instance actually a sedge—is *Carex mor-*

rowii 'Aureo-Marginata', whose gold and light green leaves keep their color all through the winter. Another carex, *C. buchananii*, is more of a novelty than a thing of beauty: its tan leaves make it seem dead at first glance, but they do have an appealing burnish or polish, and in the winter there are overtones of cranberry.

Besides their subtle colors, ornamental grasses bring to the garden the important elements of movement and sound. The taller grasses especially are playthings of the wind, gently swaying in the slightest breeze and dancing a jig in strong gusts. They also move with life when wrens and finches and other small birds choose them as a momentary perch. And the rustle of the wind through their plumes has something primordial about it. It is a sound the distant ancestors of our species must have known when they still dwelled in the grassy savannas.

IN THE EARLY years of our century, ornamental grasses enjoyed a great vogue. Gardening books of the period were filled with praise for miscanthuses and other kinds, especially when the grasses were planted along streams and ponds, but the plants fell from favor in the 1920s. Then in the 1940s in the southern and western states there occurred what might be called the great pampas grass plague. It seems that almost every suburban household grew *Cortaderia selloana*, generally a pair, placed in a perfectly senseless way in the middle of the front yard on each side of the sidewalk from the street to the door. Then everyone simultaneously woke up to the idea that matched pairs of pampas grass were silly looking, and the clumps were dug up (no easy task!) and carted off to the garbage can.

That said, it must also be added that our contemporary interest in ornamental grasses has almost nothing to do with early twentieth century horticultural traditions or the pampas grass craze of my own boyhood in Texas, and almost everything to do with the great German plantsman Karl Foerster. Foerster was passionate about grasses, which he called "the hair of Mother Earth," and he promoted their widespread use in both public and private gardens. He also selected and propagated superior forms as cultivars. His ideas and also his grasses entered American life quite recently through the efforts of three people in particular: Kurt Bluemel, Wolfgang

Oehme, and James Van Sweden—the first two born in Germany, and the third a Midwesterner. Bluemel imported to the United States a huge list of cultivars originating in Germany, which entered the nursery trade through his own nursery in Maryland. Many of their names tell the story—*Deschampsia* 'Goldschleier', *Miscanthus* 'Silberfeder', and *Molinia* 'Windspiel', for example. In their turn, Oehme and Van Sweden, two landscape architects based in Baltimore and the District of Columbia, have given many American gardens a new look that makes dramatic use of ornamental grasses. Karl Foerster's influence is apparent.

The work of Oehme and Van Sweden departs from horticultural practices of long standing in America. Lawns and foundation plantings, the most characteristic American landscaping features since the late nineteenth century, disappear almost entirely. So do the habits of mind that produce a brief orgy of springtime color followed by months of unrelieved green. In such designs as the "New American Garden," recently installed at the National Arboretum in Washington, D.C., Oehme and Van Sweden set out to show the exciting possibilities of a suburban landscape style designed to be aesthetically pleasing throughout the year. A key element in their work is fully exploiting the great diversity of form and color that ornamental grasses offer.

Sometimes we look at something without really seeing it. As Marshall McLuhan once pointed out, a fish is never really aware of water as such, because water is its element. So it is with many Americans as we look at our gardens, compare them unfavorably with those in Great Britain, and lament our inability to grow plants that our British counterparts grow with no trouble. Potentillas that are a clear red in England's mild summers are muddy in our hotter and more humid ones. To grow meconopsis, the blue Himalayan poppy, is a feasible ambition there, but here it's a recipe for frustration and despair. But gardening in America has its compensations, even relative to England, and high on the list of them is that most of the grasses that flower so splendidly here in late summer and in fall never flower in England, nor do they show much there in the way of fall color, such as the cranberry color Ravenna grass assumes in October on this side of the Atlantic. It takes a

Images of Africa's savannas are often evoked in connection with ornamental grasses, and rightly so. Here is an apt domestic pairing: a tousled and tawny carex lending a touch of wildness to a house cat in a Berkeley, California, garden.

Opposite: The purplish inflorescences of *Pennisetum alopecuroides* 'Moudry' (top), which appear in late September, much resemble woolly bear caterpillars. (Bottom) Japanese blood grass (*Imperata cylindrica* 'Rubra') is a recent import. It is especially lovely planted with blue sheep's fescue (*Festuca ovina* 'Glauca').

visitor from overseas to tell us what we've got, so I'll turn the matter over to my British friend Stephen Lacey, who wrote the following in a letter after he visited the eastern United States one October to lecture on perennials:

> The Oehme, Van Sweden gardens in Washington were looking especially effective, with the sweeps of golden rudbeckias and red sedums in full swing and contrasting with the wispy foliage and feathery plumes of pennisetum and miscanthus. Autumn must be the best time to view these. ... I was first alerted to the beauty of flowering grasses here and as I visited more gardens my notebook began to bulge with their names. Few are available in Britain (apart from the ubiquitous pampas grasses), and then only from specialist nurseries, not ordinary garden centres. The beds in front of the visitor center at the National Arboretum contained a fine array. I especially liked *Miscanthus sinensis* 'Morning Light' with narrow variegated leaves, and the erect *Calamagrostis x acutiflora* 'Stricta', but I lost my heart to *Imperata cylindrica* 'Rubra', which, with the autumn sun behind it, lived up to its name of Japanese blood grass and quite stole the show.

I have already pointed out the harmony between autumn gardens and the larger landscape because of the predominance in each of the compositae. This harmony swells all the more when the ornamental grasses have a place in the garden. Even though most of them are not indigenous, they are reminders of many native grasses that flourish along our roadsides and that add their subtle colors to the fall palette. In "Autumn Tints," written just before he died in 1862, Thoreau paid tribute to one such grass:

> The purple grass *(Eragrostis pectinacea)* is now in the height of its beauty. I remember still when I first noticed this grass particularly. Standing on a hillside near our river, I saw, thirty or forty rods off, a strip of purple half a dozen rods long, under the edge of a wood, where the ground sloped

toward a meadow. . . . On going to and examining it, I found it to be a kind of grass in bloom, hardly a foot high, with but few green blades, and a fine spreading panicle of purple flowers, a shallow, purplish mist surrounding me. Close at hand it appeared but a dull purple, and made little impression on the eye; it was even difficult to detect; and if you plucked a single plant you were surprised to find how thin it was, and how little color it had. But viewed at a distance in a favorable light, it was of a fine lively purple, flowerlike, enriching the earth. Such puny causes combine to produce these decided effects.

Autumn's sunlight makes *Miscanthus sinensis* 'Gracillimus' and other ornamental grasses glow with special brilliance.

Bamboos also have a contribution to make, provided that considerable caution is exercised in their use. Many a bamboo has been planted by many a gardener who in short order has regretted the rashness of his act. It is in the very nature of bamboos to form thick colonies. I have two bamboos, plus a plant that looks like a bamboo but technically is not. One of my bamboos I have never been able to identify, but it grows to eighteen feet, in a circular grove twenty-five feet in diameter. The light green foliage takes on a golden tint in autumn, and it persists through the winter. It is in a very far corner of the front garden, where its spreading ways have thus far—it's been fifteen years since I planted it—presented no problem. The canes sway pleasantly in a strong wind, and the leaves make an agreeable rustle. In the absence of a panda, we help keep it under control by adding it to our April bill of fare, cutting off many of the emerging shoots three inches below the ground when they are about eight inches tall. We peel them, boil them for about five minutes to remove the slightly bitter compounds they contain, and then microwave them at full blast for ten minutes. Not all parts are edible, but the soft part at the center, which is easily pulled out, is sweet and nutty.

My other bamboo I grow in an old wooden whiskey barrel on our deck to keep it under control. It is *Sasa veitchii,* and it is very handsome. Growing to about four feet, it has unusually long and broad pale green leaves. In the autumn the edges of the leaves fade to a light yellow tinged with pink, coloration that persists through the winter. Our bamboo look-alike, *Phalaris arundinacea,* or gardener's garters, also lives in a whiskey barrel. It's a graceful thing, only two feet tall, with leaves striped green and creamy white. In late spring, we pull up the outermost shoots around the clump and plant red coleus, for a splendid combination of colored foliage.

Leaves of *Miscanthus sinensis* 'Variegatus' lap up against and over a yew hedge for a dramatic effect at the Jane Watson Erwin Perennial Garden of the New York Botanical Garden. The beds here were designed with autumn specially in mind.

Annuals in the Autumn Garden

The right time and the right place to consider the role annuals play in the autumn—and the greater role that they could play, if gardeners changed a few habits of recent vintage and went back to some old practices—are spring and the local garden center. On a sunny Saturday in mid-May, the half-dozen garden centers within a twenty-minute drive of my house are busy places, their parking lots on the verge of gridlock as customers arrive to fill their trunks and backseats with their spring supply of annuals, most of them already blooming in market packs. There seems to be enough choice here to terrify an existentialist, in such apparently simple matters as deciding which among ten pink hybrid petunias will go in the window boxes. The list of annuals sold in market packs is long, including, to name the major ones, alyssum, ageratum, begonias, coleus, impatiens, annual lobelias, marigolds, red bedding salvias, and periwinkles. Here there seems to be all that's needed to make a summer garden that will linger well into fall.

There's something else here as well—the triumphant evidence of the huge success of the seed industry and its hybridizers. Since World War II, breeders have brought us new colors of petunias such as red and pale yellow, strains of coleus that don't need pinching to keep them from dying after they set seeds in midsummer, and a great many impatiens that stay compact, come in a wide range of separate colors, bloom like crazy, and prove wonderful for getting color into shady or semishady spots. More recent developments in impatiens, since the 1970s, are the New Guinea hybrids, which can take full sun, have blossoms the size of fifty-cent pieces, and boast attractive, variegated foliage. New strains of portulaca have lost their old habits of closing their flowers in late morning and of dying in midsummer. There are new annual dianthuses that bloom from early May until the temperature at night drops into the 20s and stays there—and that may return another year, as they have decidedly perennial tendencies. As for marigolds, there are new ones every year. Our range of choices of annuals seems ever richer and wider.

The hybridizers are also responsible for breeding into these annuals the trait of blooming early, when only a few inches tall. This trait offers customers the considerable advantage that we can see what we are getting, avoiding the chance of accidentally combining colors that will look horrendous together.

On a fine Saturday morning in mid-May, I am right there at my local garden center with the rest of the traffic. I have my reasons. I like the freedom and easy convenience that come from not having to start my own ageratum and wax begonias from seed. I like the chance to see what I am getting, instead of making a choice based on pictures in seed catalogues, which sometimes stretch the truth in praising what they sell.

Still, it seems clear that we could have better annuals—and more kinds—in autumn if we went a bit beyond what garden centers have to offer. Some wonderful annuals are holdouts. They have their own internal clocks and stubbornly refuse to bloom in market packs. Other annuals can't stand being transplanted and must be sown where they will bloom. Yet others wait to germinate until the soil warms up, by which time spring has passed and garden centers have no annuals left to sell except some ratty leftovers. If we allow our choices to be limited to the annuals these places sell (and what they sell is determined by what the majority of their customers want to buy, meaning that we are in the horticultural territory of the least common denominator), we limit the pleasures our gardens afford us. We need to relearn something our parents knew: to get plants, some plants at least, we need to plant seeds.

Once we have decided to grow some of our annuals from seed, in addition to those we get from the garden center in the spring, brand-new possibilities open up. A little cleverness and calculation will enable us to bring special richness and delight to the autumn garden. Late sowing is the trick. Too often when we ask "When can I plant x?" we really mean "How early can we plant x?" There's no such thing in gardening as instant gratification, but we often choose an early reward over a deferred satisfaction. In his article on annuals in the 1914 edition of his classic, three-volume reference work, *The Standard Cyclopedia of Horticulture,* Liberty Hyde Bailey wrote: "The tendency to sow everything for early bloom deprives the garden of much freshness and interest in autumn." He advised that in the latitude of New York City, a June sowing of California poppies, portulaca, mignonette, phlox, and other annuals would provide a flush of new bloom starting in September and continuing until the first frost or even the first hard freeze, depending on how tender a given plant might be. For gardens considerably farther south than New York, Professor Bailey's advice can be amended. A longer growing season permits sowing well into July, even early August.

"When can I plant x?" in other words, should also mean, "How late can I plant x?" The answer will differ from one kind of annual to the next, but the seasonal mathematics is the same. Get out the catalogue of Burpee, Park, Stokes, or one of the other seed houses that sell a wide range of annuals, and study the information about

Mixed cosmos, sown lavishly in late June, produce a pleasant meadow garden in early fall and are wonderful cut flowers.

the time it takes for specific annuals to germinate and then to come into bloom. Then figure backward from the average date of the first killing frost in your neighborhood. If it takes annual scabiosas two weeks to germinate and another two months to start a season of bloom that will be at its best for some four weeks, and if the average date of the first frost in your area is October 1, then the rough date for sowing scabiosas for September flowers is June 15. But this kind of reckoning is far from absolute. Seed houses base their dates on the basis of early sowing for midsummer bloom. In warm soils, germination may occur more quickly, and so may a plant's subsequent growth to maturity. Cool autumn nights, moreover, can stretch out the blooming season. And the average date of the first frost is only a statistic, not a reliable predictor of how the weather will actually behave.

After several decades of being a garden-center spring junky and allowing the question of what annuals I would have in my garden in the autumn to be settled by what those places sold, I mended my ways not long ago, returning to the seed catalogues and to sowing at least some seeds myself, much like people of a certain maturity who go back to the religion they abandoned when they were young. I have in the process rediscovered some old friends from childhood that don't hang out with petunias and impatiens at the local Annabelle's or Frank's garden emporium. There's cosmos, for starters, the 'Sensation' strain with its large flowers of clear pink, crimson, or white, and its airy foliage on rather noble plants that grow shoulder high. I know no finer cut flower for a mixed bouquet. There's four o'clock, like morning glories and blue flax and moonflowers, a plant that told me the time of day when I was a child. Wide and spreading, four o'clocks are charmingly old-fashioned and as variable as a calico quilt in the several colors of flowers that the same plant can produce, all opening in late afternoon and lasting until dawn. There's nigella or love-in-a-mist, with its wonderful azure flowers followed by puffed and armored seed pods. And there's annual candytuft, whose name evokes memories of cotton candy at county fairs—even if it actually comes from *Candia,* an ancient word for Crete, where it is native.

Two other plants that connect with my past are Mexican hat

Calliopsis *(Coreopsis tinctoria)* blooms unstintingly in earthy, Van Gogh colors.

(Ratibida columnifera) and calliopsis *(Coreopsis tinctoria)*, which are native to the Great Plains and to the Southwest (where they are perennials). I like to plant these daisies right next to each other for two reasons. They remind me of Texas, where since the 1930s the Highway Department has planted them, along with bluebonnets and Indian paintbrush and pink evening primroses, along more than a million acres of the state's roadsides—collectively forming the world's largest garden of wildflowers. For another, their colors mirror one another—deep golds combining with dark brownish maroons—while the forms of their flowers and foliage contrast nicely. Mexican hat, whose prominent central cone, narrow and over an inch long, gives its common name a certain inevitability, has deeply cut, almost feathery gray-green foliage. The flowers have a sweet scent that is rare in the daisy family. Calliopsis combines golden yellow and crimson and maroon, sometimes with contrasting eye-zones at the center of the circle of ray flowers. In midsummer, these colors would be a bit too torrid for comfort, but seen in September from an early June sowing, they bring a welcome and cheering warmth.

I would also like to sing the praises of one of our native southwestern zinnias. It is *Zinnia linearis,* also listed as *Z. angustifolius.* Under either name, it is a charmer, bearing a profusion of glowing apricot-orange flowers right up to frost, on plants just over a foot tall. The flowers are single, and the slender leaves, even in the South, are immune to the fungus diseases that make many hybrid strains of zinnia disgusting to behold in humid weather. I like this zinnia scattered in masses around the garden, where it can consort well with any plant with blue or purple flowers.

When it comes to the eschscholzia, or California poppy, which my mother always planted in her garden, I gladly leave the field to the nineteenth-century New England poet Celia Thaxter, for no one has written more lyrically of these (or any other plant) than she did in *An Island Garden* (1894):

> Down into the sweet plot I go and gather a few of these, bringing them to my little table and sitting down before them, the better to admire and adore their beauty. . . . One

A late sowing of California poppies produces a golden reward in the fall. My mother never failed to have these lustrous flowers in her garden in Dallas, Texas. Recent strains come in pastel shades.

blossom I take in a loving hand the more closely to examine it, and it breathes a glory of color into sense and spirit which is enough to kindle the dullest imagination. The stems and fine thread-like leaves are smooth and cool gray-green, as if to temper the fire of the blossoms, which are smooth also, unlike almost all other Poppies. . . . Every cool gray-green leaf is tipped with a tiny line of red, every flower-bud wears a little pale-green pointed cap like an elf, and in the early morning, when the bud is ready to blow, it pushes off the pretty cap and unfolds all of its loveliness to the sun. . . . It is held upright upon a straight and polished stem, its petals curving upward and outward into the cup of light, pure gold, with a lustrous satin sheen; a rich orange is painted on the gold, drawn in infinitely fine lines to a point at the centre of the edge of each petal, so that the effect is that of a diamond of flame in a cup of gold. It is not enough that the powdery anthers are orange bordered by gold; they are whirled about the very heart of the flower like a revolving Catherine-wheel of fire. In the centre of the anthers is a shining point of warm sea-green, a last, consummate touch which makes the beauty of the blossom supreme.

Mrs. Thaxter, I believe, would welcome the newer strains of California poppies, such as 'Ballerina' and 'Thai Silk', which enlarge the palette from richly burnished gold to include subtle pastel shades of pale pink, warm cream, light yellow, and carmine, as well as glowing crimsons and scarlets. Their natural season of bloom is early summer, but sown where they are to grow in the middle of June, they will flower beautifully in September.

Not all of the annuals in my fall garden are old friends. I've made some new ones, too. One of the best, and a plant I never mean to be without from now to kingdom come, is *Lavatera trimestris,* a member of the mallow family. *L. trimestris* has stunningly beautiful single blossoms like little hollyhocks, but they are borne on a mounded plant just two feet tall. I grow two sorts, both with attractive overlapping and faintly ruffled flowers. 'Mont Rose' looks

Members of the mallow family, the lavateras are recent acquaintances of mine, and I mean never to be without them. Here, 'Mont Rose' and 'Mont Blanc' command much attention, with *Verbena canadensis* and lamium holding the foreground.

pink from a distance, but up close it is much more complex in color, marked with a star of maroon at the center, with dusky-rose stripes radiating out toward the edges of the petals. It has a silvery sheen. Its sibling, 'Mont Blanc', is pure and glistening white. Only a few flowers open at a time when the plant starts blooming, but more and more appear each day for several weeks, until they almost conceal the foliage. Sow in mid-June for September flowering. Another fine recent discovery is *Nicotiana sylvestris*, mentioned in an earlier chapter but worth mentioning again. This plant, with a conical habit and lower leaves up to two feet long, grows up to six feet tall. For months on end it produces great clusters of long, tubular blossoms of pure white. The flowers are pyrotechnic, seeming to explode from the top of the plant. At night, like many but not all of the species and cultivars of flowering tobacco, its blooms are richly and sweetly fragrant. Since this plant keeps blooming over an extended season without playing out, it can be planted inside in pots in early April and set outside in mid-May. It will flower heavily from early July right through the first heavy freeze.

ALTHOUGH MANY ANNUALS can by calculated late sowing be coaxed into the height of bloom after September 1, fairly few are true autumn bloomers. But there are some. One indisputable autumn annual, and a very appealing one, is tithonia, like the dahlia a native of Mexico. It deserves to be much more widely planted than it is. For several weeks starting in late September, it is covered with scores of velvety crimson-orange single daisies about three inches across. It makes a good, long-lasting cut flower, and it usually self-seeds to return in future years. Here is one flower I wish hybridizers had left alone, but they have almost succeeded in dwarfing it. It used to be that tithonias could be counted on to top seven feet or more, but several strains now sold quit at under three feet, robbing gardeners of the pleasure of looking up at the brilliant orange blossoms against a cobalt October sky. It is good to be able to report, however, that volunteer seedlings in the second year vary from dwarf forms to their former lofty selves. By roguing the crop and pulling out any plants that show no signs of high aspirations, a determined gardener can restore what nature gave and the breeders have tried to take away.

Most of the other annuals that don't start blooming until very late summer or early fall are vines that won't germinate in cool and soggy soil and that need time to make a lot of vegetative growth before they will bloom. One of the best of these is *Cobaea scandens*, a tender perennial that in cold climates may be grown as an annual, if started inside in pots in a warm room. Germination takes up to a month, so the seeds should be sown some eight weeks before the average date of the last killing frost in spring. Also known as cup-and-saucer vine, *C. scandens* is highly popular in northern Europe but generally overlooked in America, even though it is native to Mexico. The large flowers, which resemble those of biennial campanulas, are very long lasting. They go through some fascinating changes of color as they mature. Green at first, they

For months on end *Nicotiana sylvestris* produces clusters of long, tubular blossoms, which seem to explode from the top of the plant. Here the blossoms shower down like little Roman candles on *Salvia patens* (left), *Lavatera* 'Barnsley', and tradescantia.

then turn to lavender and finally to a deep shade of purple. There is also a white form, but the purple is more desirable. Cobaea makes rapid growth once it is transplanted into the garden after the soil warms up and all danger of frost is past. The vines are dense and heavy—ideal subjects for a trellis or a pergola, provided that the wooden structure is solid and substantial enough to bear a considerable amount of weight.

Another great vine is moonflower, sometimes listed as *Ipomoea alba,* sometimes as *Calonyction aculeatum.* In the same genus as the sweet potato, this is another perennial from tropical America that may be grown in the temperate zone as an annual. When we lived in the Shenandoah Valley of Virginia, we planted the heavy seeds directly in the ground after soaking them for a few hours in lukewarm water. They germinated almost immediately, grew rapidly to become immense vines, and started flowering in late July. The tightly rolled and pleated buds begin to puff up slightly in late afternoon, and at dusk they unfurl into blossoms as white as linen, but with a silken gloss. They open quite suddenly on a warm evening, in less than a minute. Every night, more and more blossoms open, until the glossy, heart-shaped leaves are almost hidden at night. Even though my garden in New Jersey is not a great deal farther north than the place we lived in Virginia, the few degrees of latitude make a difference. Here we have to start the seeds inside in peat pots in late April, for transplanting to the garden in late May. Moonflowers require full sun and copious moisture, but lean soil is best. Too much nitrogen will produce heavy vegetative growth and few flowers. Even if I meet all of these conditions, it may be September before we see any blooms, and the vines do not flower quite as luxuriantly as they did in Virginia. Still, moonflowers own a part of my heart, and some years, when I forget to plant them in time, their absence is a palpable loss.

I've loved moonflowers since I was a child, but I recently discovered another terrific autumn vine. One fall day not long ago, when driving to work in something of a hurry, I caught a glimpse of it growing up the side of a house a couple of blocks from my own. I'd had my eye on that house anyway, because after years of its neglect and gradual descent into decrepitude, someone had moved in who started caring for it. It had gotten the first fresh coat of white paint in years. The screens had been repaired, and a broken window in the attic had been reglazed. For the first time in memory, there were some flowers, a few geraniums in a window box, nothing special, but *nice.* The vine I spotted as I drove by, however, was new to me, and even at 40 m.p.h. it was special— something like a grape, but with clusters of purple flowers atop the stems.

I couldn't stop for a closer look, but that night Hella and I wandered over, introduced ourselves to the young couple who had moved in, and said some admiring words about the vine. It wasn't a grape, which was no surprise. The slightly purplish leaves were three-lobed. The large pealike blossoms, purple from a distance, were more elegantly colored up close, washed with tones of pink and grayish mauve. Borne in a long cluster like wisteria flowers, but upright instead of hanging, they had the keels and standards that unmistakably put them in the legume family. But I had no idea what legume the plant was. My new neighbors knew only that a friend had given them the seeds to plant. They had no idea whether it was an annual or a perennial.

The next morning, I called a friend with that special gift of being able to identify plants from the vaguest, "sort of like this, sort of like that," mumblings of a description. After a couple of questions, she said the strange words, *Dolichos lablab,* then added that botanists had recently decided it was really *Dipogon lablab.* Its common names include velvet bean, bonavista vine, hyacinth bean, and lablab bean. In the tropics, the plant is used for food. Humans eat the protein-rich pods and seeds, and its leaves provide excellent forage for cattle. In North America it has been grown as an ornamental annual since at least the eighteenth century; Thomas Jefferson thought highly of it and planted it widely at Monticello.

The highest glory of the lablab bean, it turns out, is not the flowers, lovely though they may be. After they fade and drop off, the foliage smolders into a darker purple. The seed pods lengthen and swell, and they glow like rubies in the autumn sun. The show, alas, is not a long one, for this remarkable bean is extremely tender. The faintest touch of frost blackens the vines overnight. Still, the

Lablab beans are among the indispensable annuals of autumn, first for their spikes of lavender-purple blossoms, then for their smoky-toned foliage and their large and burnished seed pods. They grow at Montrose Nursery on a long fence in front of the lath house.

This riot of late-season flowers and foliage is punctuated by the white blossoms of tall *Nicotiana sylvestris.* Of even greater stature is Joe Pye weed, whose dusky, old rose flowers can be seen behind the nicotiana. Also in bloom are perovskia, whose silvery-blue flower spikes seem to dance across the scene; *Achillea* 'Coronation Gold'; *Verbena bonariensis* (left of the nicotiana); and *Lobelia cardinalis.*

The tropical vine *Mandevilla* 'Alice DuPont' must be brought inside in the winter before the first killing freeze, but it produces a heavy crop of large glowing pink blossoms from midsummer right up to the first frost.

show is beautiful while it lasts, and it's good to know that both Burpee and Park offer the seeds in their catalogues.

A final vine worth seeking out is mandevilla, another tropical vine, but one that may be brought inside during the winter as a houseplant. I am lucky enough to live near a greenhouse nursery which sells many tropical plants, including mandevillas, to local customers; Logee's Greenhouses does offer this fairly rare plant in its mail-order catalogue. A mature plant will bloom continuously from May to October, but a small rooted cutting will start blooming in August. There are two worthy sorts, *Mandevilla sanderi* and *M. x* 'Alice DuPont'. *M. sanderi* has glossy leaves with a bronze cast and long, tapering buds that open into deep rose-pink flowers that look somewhat like petunias, but much more elegant. 'Alice Du-Pont', which was hybridized at Longwood Gardens, in Kennett Square, Pennsylvania, as a complicated cross among several species native to South America, bears huge, thick leaves that are ribbed and very leathery, and stunning large flowers of luminous soft pink. We grow both during the summer in hanging baskets on our deck, where they grow up into the canopy of hardy kiwi vines covering the pergola. An oddity of this plant is the latex of its sap, which seals off the stems when they are cut. When we prune 'Alice DuPont' back before bringing it inside, the stems continue to bloom for several weeks above the deck, despite a missing root system. Seen from our bedroom window upstairs, the flowers are wonderful to behold.

A VERY CLOSE friend of mine who has gardened for years the easy way, ordering her perennials from nurseries and picking up her annuals each spring at Annabelle's, planted her first seeds not long ago. There were some perennials, like columbines and hollyhocks, but she also planted a few annuals, mostly calendulas. The day the first seedlings appeared she asked me to drop by and take a look at them. I did, but I also took a look at her. Her eyes were merry, she wore a broad and happy smile, and she glowed with surprise and pleasure. "I did it," she said, "I planted some seeds, and they actually came up for me." After a slight pause, she added, "I think everybody should plant seeds. It gives a sense of real connection with life."

I agree, but here I would like to call attention to one of the facts of our national horticultural life—the steadily diminishing number of different kinds of seeds sold in such places as grocery and hardware stores in the consignment racks of companies like Ferry-Morse, Northrup-King, and Burpee. Every year the selection grows slimmer and slimmer, and it's been a very long time since I've seen the seeds of candytuft in a store where I might buy them on impulse during an errand to buy eggs and milk or a new pruning saw. It's those easy habits we have fallen into. If grocery stores aren't selling many seeds, it's bound to be that customers have stopped buying them. In the garden center, of course, there's a better selection of seeds, but even there the number seems to be steadily diminishing. We can no longer drive a few minutes, when the mood is on us to plant morning glory or candytuft or cleome seeds, with any assurance that we will come home with them. We have to take the extra trouble, even with annuals once very common, to study a catalogue, fill out an order sheet, mail it to a seed company, and then wait until the postman brings our order, by which time the impulse to plant

A late sowing of annuals can produce a summery look even in late September, as here in a California garden.

morning glories may have passed or it may no longer be the right time.

It was not always thus. My first job, when I was twelve, was working Saturdays, and late afternoons on school days, at the Nicholson Seed Company in the Dallas suburb of Highland Park. An entire wall of the front part of the store was devoted to little bins containing seed packages of hundreds of different kinds of annuals and perennials, as well as a few vegetables. (Highland Park was not exactly vegetable territory, and still isn't.) The wall with its little bins stretched some sixty feet, and I recall the impression it made on me: the plant kingdom is very vast and very diverse, and not even many lifetimes would be sufficient to embrace it all. That wall of bins and their seeds was in fact a kind of sermon, and one we must need to hear. Powerful forces are at work in this world to constrict the diverse forms of life it contains. Many varieties of vegetables and their germ plasm are being threatened by a much lesser number of hybrids—which bring short-term profit but threaten long-term loss. Family farms that once supported agricultural diversity are now becoming vast monocultures of wheat or corn or soybeans. Population pressures in the world's tropical regions, combined with exploitation of their resources, are contributing to the loss of whole species of plants and animals on an unimaginable scale and with unimaginable speed. Sensible people who realize these things will want to bear witness against them. One person, perhaps, can't do very much, but one person can do what one person can do. It may be something small. Bedding salvias and marigolds, to go back to the beginning, are themselves monocultures. Someone who plants in a late sowing some annual or other that no one else in town is growing—and plants it where it is visible to passing neighbors and strangers—is bearing a small witness to our need to preserve the richness of life on this planet, not diminish it.

Some Woody Plants of Autumn

The most significant decisions in making a garden—those that will bring pleasure or despair or boredom for years after they are made—concern the choice of woody plants, the trees and shrubs that will as they mature give shape, texture, character, and volume or mass to the garden that is made. In addition to being grown as specimens interesting in their own right, woody plants are also of great value as visual screens, ensuring that to be enjoyed the garden must be walked through and experienced with all the senses, not just taken in as a whole with a glance. As screens, these all-important plants provide a garden with its element of mystery and surprise, as when you walk around a large shrub rose and discover that colchicums have opened since yesterday evening.

It follows that selecting these essential plants with care is a matter of great moment and importance. For one thing, although even a fairly small garden can accommodate an amazingly large number of bulbs and annuals and perennials, even a fairly large one can accommodate only a limited number of shrubs and trees. Errors in judgment are hard to hide. It is possible to make dreadful mistakes with herbaceous perennials, of course. I have done so repeatedly, and sometimes spectacularly, as when an orange oriental poppy got a spot right next to a magenta *Lychnis coronaria*, a combination not soon forgotten or forgiven. But herbaceous plants can be moved around easily. The wrong location this year can become the right one next year. If need be, plants can be tried in successive locations for several years until they're right. And if a perennial is an unredeemably bad choice, it can be ripped out and consigned to the compost pile. Woody plants are far less tractable, offering much less chance to correct mistakes later on. There are only two choices about an oak tree forty feet high: leave it alone, or cut it down. Shrubs are easier to remove or cut back and transplant to a new location, but there's hard work involved. Only recently I had to take out a mock orange that I had planted thoughtlessly just four years back, giving no consideration to how large it would become or to how it would shade one corner of the deck that we wanted to keep sunny. It took six hours with shovel, pick, ax, and crowbar to get it out, and I ached for days. The thought didn't help that it took under ten minutes to plant it in the first place.

It may also be noted that, except among devoted gesneriadophiles and members of the American Rock Garden Society so far gone in their quest for little alpines that they regard anyone who has a decent word to say about any plant more than three inches high as way beyond the pale, woody plants call forth some of the deepest affections of all. (I make here the usual disclaimer about some of my best friends being rock gardeners. It happens to be true.) I have a spry friend, a little lame of body, but rich in spirit and passion, who polishes her crape myrtles every fall, something she's been doing for about seventy years. She climbs up a step ladder, strips off the peeling reddish brown bark, and gets going with a flannel rag until the trunks take on a sober glow, like polished ivory, except light beige in color. And the plants I remember best from boyhood are a vitex and a white peach tree into which I could climb and read. The peach offered the dividend of delicious fruit at hand.

I would hate to have to start a garden from absolute scratch, as one of our sons is doing around his new house in the middle of a large lot in Pennsylvania that used to be part of a cornfield. But I understand the psychology that goes with the territory. The first priority is putting in a lawn. Next come trees and shrubs, as many as the budget can afford and the bigger the better, generally from a local nursery or garden center. The main idea is to get rid of the naked look of a new house surrounded by nothing but turf. And the upshot is that a few years later the result of all the frantic planting is boring. There will be arborvitae, junipers, Japanese black pines, and all the other conifers the neighbors have also planted. There will be some quick-growing maples, and lots of euonymus. And there will be a great number of woody plants that bloom in the spring—forsythias, white or pink dogwoods, saucer magnolias, and of course azaleas and rhododendrons. The flood of color in April and May will pass quickly, followed by a tide of unrelieved green. Spring is the only season taken into serious account in this habitual style of landscaping.

Those of us who move into houses other people have owned before us often find a collection of woody plants assembled in the same way. We also may discover worse mistakes than a simple lack of imagination. My own garden offers several examples. Apart from two very handsome juniper trees at least a century old and standing eighty feet high, the largest woody plants I live with are two black cherry trees at one side of the house and a swamp maple out back. I cannot imagine anything worse. The cherries rain down thousands of messy little fruits every year in late summer, and the seedlings germinate everywhere the next spring. The swamp maple, ancient now and perhaps near its end, contributes its own abundant progeny to the chore of spring weeding, and its shallow roots run throughout the garden, competing with other plants for nutrients and water. As for the old hedge of purple lilacs, I am not at all sentimental about them. They bloom for two weeks only, and most of the summer they are covered with the unsightly bloom of mildew. One of these days, they will be removed.

It would be a great improvement in the nation's gardening if we all thought more carefully about woody plants. Except that it would be a flagrant transgression of the right to privacy and the right to plant azaleas if you want to, I wouldn't mind seeing an ordinance enjoining the owners of new houses on naked lots to wait a year before they planted a single shrub or tree after they get the lawn in, requiring them meanwhile to visit specialty nurseries, study nursery catalogues, and go to a good arboretum once a month to see which plants merit attention in seasons other than spring. While I'm imagining this oppressive piece of legislation, I might as well set up a new political office, the Commissar of Plant Diversity. It would be this person's job to see to it that every front yard in a given neighborhood had one tree and one shrub in it that none of the neighbors was growing. There could be a directory of plants and their owners, so that everyone would know that the Joneses had a *Betula maximowicziana* and the Smiths a *Philadelphus pekinensis.* The effect would be to make a neighborhood itself an arboretum.

Legislation being improper, I can only stand up and urge that we ask some penetrating questions about plants, and that we require more out of them than simply taking up room and carrying on photosynthesis. I am increasingly convinced, furthermore, that except in gardens of very considerable size there is little place for any woody plant that offers only a brief splash of color in high spring, no matter how pretty a splash it may be. I take the view that there's no need for me to plant the shrubs and trees that flower so gloriously if briefly every spring. My neighbors have done it for me. I don't need forsythias, since a plant census would show three of them for every human inhabitant in town. They are fully on view in the front gardens of the neighborhood, and I see as many of them as I wish whenever I drive to the grocery store for milk and cat food. I also see enough azaleas this way to do me for the year. (One massed planting down the street is especially noteworthy for its combination of popsicle shades of pink, scarlet, and orange. I always wonder if it's the result of unusual verve on the part of the azaleas' owner or of a severe need for him to have his eyes checked.) In my neighborhood rambles, I can note each spring the slight variations in the onset of bloom in the Japanese cherries. In some years, I observe with pleasure that all of the pink magnolias in town managed to escape the late frost that usually turns their petals to a disgusting brown mush. I borrow my neighbors' gardens and the springtime joys they offer the passerby.

MEANWHILE I AM free to seek out for myself other woody plants with more to offer than bright color in spring, and I have some standards. Better put, certain woody plants that I have lived with on terms of some intimacy over the years set the standards by which others may be judged. The main question is one of enduring interest. Is a plant interesting only briefly, or does it please, for one reason or another, for more than one season?

The sourwood tree *(Oxydendrum arboreum)* is an excellent example of a plant that passes every test. Its spring foliage is a good and glossy fresh green, and it blooms for several weeks in early summer, bearing clusters of small white flowers, somewhat reminiscent of lily-of-the-valley. The autumn foliage is a spectacularly warm shade of red, and the tree is admirable even in winter for its persistent dried seed heads, which have always reminded me of outstretched hands. It is one of the very best of our native trees, and its moderate size keeps it in scale for a garden of modest proportions. (In the wild, it can reach anywhere from sixty to seventy-five feet, but it takes decades to do so.)

Two other touchstone plants are hydrangeas. I would not want to be without the old-fashioned *Hydrangea paniculata* 'Grandiflora'—pee-gee, for short. Our one plant of pee-gee is part of a boundary hedge along the back side of our property, grown in what some might call a tapestry, others a mess, of other plants—eastern dogwoods, rugosa roses, and several white pines which, though now forty feet high, still retain most of their lower branches. This hydrangea is much used in my neighborhood as a freestanding shrub or small tree in front gardens, and to fairly pleasant effect. But my own specimen, although lopsided, seems especially fine growing intermingled with a tangle of other plants. The panicles or large clusters of bracts, several dozen bracts per cluster, creamy

If I could plant only one tree, I can easily name it—our native sourwood *(Oxydendron arboreum)*. Its fall foliage and seed heads are stunning together, but sourwood is excellent in any season, including winter, when its seeds lend continuing textural interest.

white in late summer, are subtly colored almost beyond description in October, before they take on the light parchment hue they will wear through most of the winter. On the tops of the panicles, where sunlight strikes them directly, they are a deep shade of old-rose. The bracts on the bottoms of the panicles are a ghostly shade of lime, tending toward pale cream. In the intermediate bracts, these two colors blend in different degrees, so subtly that no two bracts are identical. The plant in its upper reaches grows into and through the branches of a white pine. The combination of the blue-green needles of the pine and the old-rose and lime-cream of the hydrangea was not arrived at by design—but then, accidental delight is one of the main joys of gardening. There is another cultivar of *H. paniculata*, called 'Tardiva', which is also worth seeking out. It blooms in September, and its flower heads, being smaller and lighter than those on pee-gee, do not have the demerit of overburdening the bush.

The oak-leaved hydrangea *(H. quercifolia)* is virtually indispensable for its large and showy clusters of white flowers and its ability to bloom in either full sun or fairly deep shade. It was discovered in 1773 in Georgia by William Bartram, who named it and called it "a very singular and beautiful shrub." He then went on with a more detailed description, writing in his *Travels* (1792) that

> It grows in coppices or clumps near or on the banks; . . . the stems divide regularly or oppositely, though the branches are crooked or wreathe about horizontally and then again divide, forming others which terminate with large heavy panicles or thyrsi of flowers; but these flowers are of two kinds: the numerous partial spikes which compose the panicles and consist of a multitude of very small fruitful flowers, terminate with one or more very large expansive neutral or mock flowers, standing on a large, slender, stiff peduncle; these flowers are composed of four broad oval petals or segments, of a dark rose or crimson colour at first, but as they become older acquire a deeper red or purplish hue, and lastly are of a brown or ferruginous colour.

If I could plant only one shrub, it would again be a North American native, *Hydrangea quercifolia*. Its creamy panicles of flowers and bracts in summer are surpassingly beautiful, and in the fall its leaves show virtually every tint of the autumn palette.

The autumn foliage of the oak-leafed hydrangea is a good shade of coppery red brushed with wine, and the dried panicles persist into winter and beyond, making this native American shrub a plant for all seasons. Although the species or type is superb as it is, I also like a double cultivar called 'Snowflake'. The hose-in-hose tier of bracts open lime green, changing to cream and then to rose-tan. As the peak season of bloom begins in August, the bracts at the base of each floret are green, while those at the front are creamy white, for a striking two-toned look. The panicles are so heavy that they droop sharply downward, like clusters of enormous grapes. A good source is Woodlanders.

I am also keen on another native, the northern bayberry *(Myrica pensylvanica)*, which I grow as a tall hedge in one part of our front garden. (In the wild, where it grows near the dunes of a nearby bay of the Atlantic Ocean, it reaches only six or seven feet high, but in more fertile soil it stretches up over twelve feet.) The leaves turn a fine brown-purple in the fall, but the berries are the thing—pewter in color, with a texture like those Fourth of July sparklers of childhood memory, they have a delicious fragrance. Used by our colonial forebears for making candles (a fact that gives me huge respect for our colonial forebears' patience and fortitude, considering the slender yield of wax in bayberries), they smell to me like Christmas, when cheap tallow candles or their petrochemical substitutes are beneath consideration.

There are many other plants whose berries in the fall and winter make them splendid candidates for inclusion in any garden. I need hardly mention the several cultivars of pyracantha or firethorn, since these are so commonly known and grown. So are the various species of cotoneaster, although I greatly admire *Cotoneaster apiculatus*, the cranberry cotoneaster, for its low and spreading habit, its pinkish white flowers in late May, its huge crop of sparkling red fruits in autumn, and its handsome evergreen foliage in winter. I grow it as a ground cover, letting it swirl beneath other plants, including a tall and airy ornamental grass, *Stipa gigantea.* It roots easily as it grows, producing by layering new plants that I can use in new locations or share with friends and neighbors.

The evergreen hollies are frankly starting to bore me just a bit, but I will put in a word for two hollies that are not quite so familiar. These are the deciduous native hollies *Ilex decidua* and *I. verticillata,* or winterberry, both knockouts for their huge crops of brilliant red fruits, which light up even the dullest day in late autumn and which persist long into winter. The berries of *I. decidua* turn red several weeks before those of other hollies. Up close, they gleam like tiny scarlet Christmas lights, but from a distance the tree or shrub—it can be grown either way, depending on pruning—is a soft haze of rosy red. This superior holly is one of the least temperamental plants I know. It tolerates shade or sun, a dry location or a moist one. It is bone hardy (to Zone 5), and it takes the hot southern summer in its stride.

Another plant outstanding for its fruit is a cultivar of our native aronia or chokeberry called 'Brilliantissima'. I also much admire several callicarpas for their berries in November, after the leaves fall. I have three planted together as a group. Two, the American beautyberry *(Callicarpa americana)* and its Korean counterpart, *C. dichotoma,* are virtually indistinguishable. Both have a heavy crop of berries best described as gunmetal blue-purple. The third, *C. japonica* 'Leucocarpa' bears in profusion small white berries on somewhat arching stems. One fine trait of callicarpas for gardeners with limited space is that they need not be allowed to hog territory. Left to themselves, they will spread up to five feet wide and high, but they can be sheared back almost to the ground annually in late winter. The treatment keeps them in bounds, and they seem to fruit more heavily with this harsh regimen.

Many of the viburnums do double duty, producing white or pink blossoms, often fragrant, in the spring, and bright red or black fruits in the fall persisting into winter. One viburnum that I prize especially, *Viburnum plicatum* 'Mariesii', does triple duty. Our fifteen-year-old plant now stands twenty feet tall, and we have trained it so that it and a Russian olive together form a high arch over the driveway. It is a splendid sight in late May when its tabulated, or horizontal, branches are covered with pure white bracts lasting well over two weeks. The huge crop of fruits the size and color of cinnamon redhots are usually gobbled up by birds in

After leaf-fall, the berries of *Ilex verticillata* glisten and gleam like polished rubies. And they go on gleaming long into winter.

A massed planting of heavenly bamboo *(Nandina domestica),* which neither hails from paradise nor is a bamboo, nevertheless provides a splendid screen to lend privacy, and the colorful autumn foliage persists through most of the winter. The graceful shrubs grow to about five feet.

midsummer before they ripen and turn black, but their cranberry-colored stalks or pedicels persist into autumn. From a distance the plant at this time still looks like it's in bloom, thanks to the strong red color against the green foliage. This shrub is still wonderful in November, when the leaves turn to a deep maroon and occasional unseasonable flowers appear here and there on its graceful branches, looking much like giant flakes of snow.

But in the autumn, of all woody plants with berries, it is a highly elegant shrub, *Nandina domestica,* or heavenly bamboo, that truly owns my heart. The common name carries only poetic truth, since it hails from China, not paradise, and it's not a bamboo at all but a member of the barberry family.

Growing some five feet tall, the nandina is a graceful shrub, with attractive compound leaves in tiers, like the stories of a pagoda. The glossy dark green foliage is handsome in the summer and even more so in the late fall and winter when it turns to a glowing shade of garnet. In midsummer it produces great sprays of waxy cream flowers, followed usually by dark crimson berries, which remain on the plant until spring. The berries make a handsome winter arrangement combined with the silver gray of sprays of dried lavender leaves and the rich mahogany of the plumes of astilbe seed heads. In the nandina's year, there's not a single dull day.

I wouldn't push my luck by trying to grow nandinas in the inland regions of the Northeast—they may survive, but often without producing flowers or fruit—but they are extremely vigorous in the Southeast, and they do well in coastal areas of the Middle Atlantic states. Nandinas are virtually immune to injury from disease or insects. They aren't bothered by drought, and in fact do well in rather dry soil. They will grow in full sun or in partial shade.

The nandina, however, was the victim of its own success earlier in this century. It was so nearly a perfect landscaping plant that it grew in American gardens by the millions and probably the billions in the 1950s and 1960s. Becoming rather too much of a very good thing, it fell from public favor and almost dropped out of the nursery trade.

Nandinas are back now, with some new wrinkles. Only one

Although nandina berries are generally dark crimson or garnet, they occasionally occur in other colors, as here, where they are yellowish cream.

genus and species is grown—*N. domestica.* But there's some diversity within the species. Occasionally the berries are white or yellow. The winter coloration of the foliage may be green instead of crimson, and there are also golds and yellows and maroons and purples. There are genes that produce dwarfism. Breeders in England, California, and New Zealand have taken advantage of all these characteristics to produce new lines of nandinas.

Among these, I've liked several well enough to add them to my garden. 'Atropurpurea Nana' is low, under two feet high, and it doesn't look much like a nandina at all, especially since it produces no flowers. In the winter, particularly when there's snow on the ground, it looks like a bonfire, with gold and red leaves on the same plant. Planted in a mass, it makes a spectacular ground cover. Another fine ground cover is 'Harbor Dwarf'. It looks just like the more familiar nandina of a generation ago, and it flowers and fruits, but it's only two feet tall. Spreading by underground runners, a few plants will quickly fill in an area. 'Royal Princess' is tall and commanding, as its name implies, but its leaves are very narrow and feathery. I have planted all of these new nandinas quite close to one another, in a single bed, so that I can observe and enjoy them. I have not, however, started talking to them, although traditional lore in Japan holds that telling nandinas about your troubles is an infallible remedy against nightmares.

SOME DESIRABLE WOODY plants contribute to a long season of interest through their variegated or colored foliage all during the growing season. The older I get, the farther I stray from the kindergarten Crayola-box mentality that says if it's a leaf, reach for a green crayon. On the other hand, I would not want to have a garden where there was not a green leaf in sight and no flowers. It seems clear that green leaves should dominate the landscape and that flowers should provide most of the changing parade of colors, until tupelos and sumacs turn to flame in late summer to announce that the autumn spectacle of brilliant foliage is about to begin. The glory of our American deciduous forests results from the decline of photosynthesis, as chlorophyll vanishes, revealing xanthophyll, carotene, and the other bright pigments the leaves have kept con-

Usually planted for the sake of its flowerlike bracts in late spring, the foliage and fruits of the Asian dogwood *(Cornus kousa)* give it great value in fall as well.

The small, single, deep-pink flowers of *Rosa glauca* in early summer teeter on the edge of insignificance, but its smoky-purple foliage and its dark, almost black-red hips redeem it altogether.

cealed all during the growing season. Nevertheless, long before autumn washes our woodlands with its tints, a considerable amount of color—gold, yellow, chartreuse, white, smoky reds and purples—may come from the foliage of certain woody plants, as well as herbaceous ones such as hostas. Ordinary dogwood, or *Cornus florida,* is lovely enough for its white or pink or red bracts in May, the delicate shade of green of its leaves in summer and their port wine tones in fall, and its dark scarlet fruits in October, but two quite special cultivars with wonderfully changeable variegated foliage are now becoming widely available. 'Cherokee Daybreak', with white bracts, bears green foliage with light cream margins, turning rose, purple, and red in mid-autumn. The leaves of its companion, 'Cherokee Sunset', which has red bracts, are splashed with glowing yellow during the summer, changing to cerise, purple, and bronze. And need I mention the Asian species *C. kousa* 'Chinensis'? Its leaves change to their autumn colors a week or two later than the native American *C. florida.* My own plant, partially shaded by an old juniper tree, turns flamboyant red on the south side, apricot gold on the north—a trick of the angle of the sun, I assume. The pale red fruits are edible but insipid, so I leave them for the birds to gobble up, as they do with evident greed and relish as soon as they start to ripen. This Chinese species, incidentally, is resistant to the strange maladies that have recently sickened and sometimes killed a good many specimens of our native *C. florida* in the northeastern states—a blight that some authorities attribute to anthracnose disease, others to stress caused by drought and high summer temperatures.

Also worth a trial are several variegated forms of *Elaeagnus pungens,* although this shrub with strong evergreen tendencies isn't reliably winter hardy much above Zone 7. The most common variety, 'Aurea', bears leaves blending creamy yellow with a soft shade of gray-green. Somewhat harder to find, but worth the search, is 'Tricolor', with foliage blending pale pink, light yellow, and olive green. But the true contribution of this plant to the fall garden is the sweet spice of its inconspicuous flowers. On an October day in North Carolina I have caught traces of it from a plant the length of a football field away. The fragrance is one that carries a great distance without losing its character, and in this regard it resembles Japanese honeysuckle and certain wisterias. It lacks the cloying, bathroom-freshener quality of the much hardier *E. angustifolia,* or Russian olive. Up close, its inconspicuous flowers smell like gardenias.

Purple foliage of any sort has a calming effect, but I have a special fondness for several plants in particular. One is the common purple-leafed plum (*Prunus cerasifera* 'Atropurpurea'), whose leaves have a distinctly reddish tint. The tree tends to be unusually short lived, but it is widely propagated and sold by many local nurseries at prices reasonable enough so that specimens can be replaced when they give up the ghost. I also like a redbud *(Cercis*

On a bright morning after a calm but frosty night, the leaves of red Japanese maples may fall to form a pool of dramatic color.

canadensis) called 'Forest Pansy', with foliage that veers almost toward black, and I am much impressed with a purple-leafed hazelnut, *Corylus avellana* 'Maxima Purpurea', which forms a large and spreading shrub about ten feet high. And there is one rose I grow just for its misty grayish purple foliage. Formerly *Rosa rubrifolia*, it now goes around as *R. glauca.* In full sun, the leaves are more purple than in partial shade.

But my absolute favorite shrub for purple foliage is purple smoke bush, or *Cotinus coggygria* 'Purpureus'. Superior cultivars are 'Velvet Cloak' and 'Royal Purple'. Left to themselves, these will become somewhat spreading shrubs, eight to ten feet high. I keep my plants pruned, however, to about three feet and grow them in a mixed border of perennials and small shrubs, with lambs ears at their feet. Purple smoke bush has a wonderful radiance that seems to emanate from the plant when it catches the golden light of early morning or late afternoon. Its color is especially fine with orange-red or bronze chrysanthemums, and it combines well with *Berberis thunbergii* 'Rosy Glow'.

Most of these purple-leafed woody plants, and others as well, such as red-leafed Japanese maples, respond sharply to regional differences in summer temperatures. In the lower reaches of Zone 7 and farther south, their rich color in spring washes out toward green as the weather gets warmer. J. C. Raulston says that the culprit is high temperatures at night, causing the sugars that are responsible for the purple pigmentation to be burned up by increased respiration.

Purple, like gray, harmonizes with every other color, and there can hardly be too much of it in a garden. Yellow, gold, and chartreuse, however, are more difficult to site, and in the case of each, a little goes a long way, especially considering the prominence of yellow shades in the flowers of many annuals and perennials. Yellow foliage also carries with it a hint of iron chlorosis and other maladies, and I believe the way to use it is with a touch of daring, the way you grasp nettles firmly to avoid their sting. What is merely *yellowish* in woody plants is best avoided in favor of franker and more definite tones. For a touch of yellow and closely related hues, I suggest European red elder (*Sambucus racemosa* 'Plumosa

Aurea'), *Viburnum opulus* 'Aureum', both richly golden, and *V. setigerum,* a strong chartreuse. Both these viburnums have great flair for the contrast between their foliage and their bright red berries. I am sometimes tempted by *Spiraea japonica* 'Goldflame', which is gold much of the season, but I have resisted, knowing that the pinkish red flowers in early summer clash sharply with the foliage.

AUTUMN IS NOT especially rich with woody plants in bloom, but there are a few. The pink ornamental cherry sold in the nursery trade as *Prunus subhirtella* 'Autumnalis', which may in fact be 'Rosea', obliges by blooming once in the spring and repeating the performance in autumn. It has a delightful if faint odor of marzipan. *Franklinia altamaha* is a small tree that gardeners came peri-

There comes a time in every garden when flowers finally give way to fall foliage as the dominant element. The careful selection of small trees and shrubs will bring added splendor, as here, with the distinctive yellow leaves of hamamelis set against the rich glow of a Japanese maple.

lously close to not knowing at all. It disappeared in the wild soon after William Bartram discovered it in Georgia and named it for Benjamin Franklin the year after the Declaration of Independence was signed. It blooms steadily if not prodigiously for a month starting in late August. The sweetly fragrant white blossoms look much like single camellias, and the bronze-red foliage sets them off with considerable pizzazz. Several cultivars of the gray-foliaged small shrub *Caryopteris x clandonensis,* ranging in color from the light blue of 'Blue Mist' to the almost purple of 'Dark Knight', stay in bloom for about five weeks in early autumn. Bees adore it. When I walk by, the shrub itself seems to be buzzing.

While I would never want to limit my own garden to a collection of native North American plants, I understand completely the passions of a few friends who lean in that direction. "Neglected" is the adjective that often precedes the phrase "native American plants," and the neglect is far too common to be ignored. I must plead mea culpa in the case of our autumn witch hazel *(Hamamelis virginiana),* which I didn't come to know until I was nearly fifty. This witch hazel begins its own long season of bloom in October, its bright gold flowers opening when the plant is still clad in its softer gold leaves, mottled with tan. The bloom continues after the foliage vanishes, and it has a fragrance that is sometimes prominent, sometimes elusive. In *The Fragrant Path* (1932), Louise Beebe Wilder wrote: "Often have I followed a scent up the breeze on a sharp autumn day to find at the end of the quest a Witch Hazel thicket, or even a single tree, in its quaint regalia. When you draw near and thrust your nose among the blossoms you perceive little or no perfume unless you crush them, but withdraw and go about other affairs and the sweetest air will overtake and envelop you." This native shrub or small tree is sharp-shooting as well as sweet-smelling. It can suddenly eject its ripe seeds with surprising power, to a distance as great as forty feet. I have never personally beheld this wonder or been struck by the plant's shrapnel, but I have seen accounts of it. Writing in the late nineteenth century in a book called *Sharp Eyes,* the American naturalist W. Hamilton Gibson stated he got a direct hit from a witch hazel: "I was suddenly stung on the cheek by some missile, and the next instant shot in the eye by another, the mysterious marksman having apparently let off both barrels of his little gun directly in my face. I soon discovered him, an army of them—in fact a saucy legion—all grinning with open mouths and white teeth exposed, and their double-barrelled guns loaded to the muzzle and ready to shoot whenever the whim should take them."

I have recently learned to place great value on a wonderful group of plants, the *x* darleyensis heaths, hybrids between the winter heath *(Erica carnea)* and the Mediterranean heath *(E. erigena)*. Evergreen shrubs that grow about eighteen inches high and spread eventually to three feet, they start blooming in mid-November, and they keep it up until the last flowers on our lilacs turn brown in May. I would treasure them even if their only real contribution were to permit the boast that I have something in bloom a full 365 days a year, but they are lovely as well as dogged. A mature plant produces many hundreds of pendant little egg-shaped flowers. 'Mediterranean White' (also sold as 'Alba' and 'Silberschmeltze') has creamy white blossoms, and 'Mediterranean Pink' (also called 'Darley Dale') has rose ones. 'Arthur Johnson', 'Furzey', and 'Ghost Hills' are all slightly different shades of lilac-pink, and 'Jack H. Brummage' is heliotrope purple. I have all these heaths planted near one another, intermingled with various cultivars of summer-blooming heather *(Calluna vulgaris)*, some of which have attractive gold or gray foliage for added interest. Certain of these heathers also undergo attractive changes in foliage as autumn arrives. The bright yellow leaves of *C. vulgaris* 'Aureafolia' turn red with the first frost. 'Robert Chapman', gold in the summer, changes to orange. And the pale yellow leaves, tipped with orange, of 'Sir John Charrington' turn deep red once really cold weather sets in. Except for June, there's always something in bloom in this part of the garden. As 'Tib', the last of our heathers, finishes blooming in November, 'Mediterranean White', the first of the heaths, has begun to chime in.

As with perennials and also annuals, a good many shrubs of summer linger in bloom into autumn. Six especially deserve to be singled out. Abelias, which are virtually trouble-free shrubs (they may die back to the roots in Zone 6 or colder, but they regenerate quickly in the spring, and they bloom on new wood), flower from late May to well after the first killing frost. The reddish brown glossy foliage is handsome, and the crop of little hanging trumpet flowers is abundant. The most common form, *Abelia x grandiflora*, bears pale pink, almost white, blossoms. 'Edward Goucher', rarer but worth the search, has larger flowers of pale lilac, and it is quite striking planted with caryopteris. 'Francis Mason', with pink flowers, develops attention-catching gold-variegated foliage when in light shade. Another lingerer is vitex, commonly called chaste tree for reasons I cannot straighten out. (Legend holds that it has aphrodisiacal properties. Legend also holds that it so reduces the libido that it was a staple drug in monasteries, whence comes another common name, monk's pepper. I follow David Hume here; where there is contradictory evidence, the judgment remains suspended.)

Many of the butterfly bushes or buddleias keep flowering into October. I grow several, but I am especially partial to 'White Profusion', whose name says it all, and to 'Lochinch', with grayish leaves colored silver on their undersides, blue-lavender blossoms with contrasting apricot throats, and a heavy, sweet fragrance that neither people nor Monarch butterflies can ignore.

I've never seen a Monarch or any other butterfly near the shrubby savory, *Satureja georgiana,* which also goes about under the aliases *Clinopodium georgianum* and *C. carolinianum.* Our house cats, however, pounce upon it with such dispatch that they destroyed many a mixed bouquet until we learned our lesson and just left it in the garden. This low shrub, some two feet tall, begins blooming in June, albeit sparsely. The tiny blossoms are a clean and uncomplicated pink to the naked eye, but the Eschenbach 10X hand lens I use to take a closer look at little things reveals them to be spotted with purple and suffused with white around their downy throats. When crushed, their leaves have a slightly minty scent. The scanty crop of flowers in summer would make this savory only a minor player in the garden, but in early October it begins to bloom profusely, with many dozens of foxglovelike blossoms all up and down its erect stems. The flowering continues well after the first frost, when the oval leaves turn to deep purple that harmonizes perfectly with the pink of the flowers. This plant wants very well-drained soil, so it is completely happy in my sandy garden. In heavy clay, it may be difficult. If the foliage goes yellow, it's a sign to add chelated iron and to lighten the soil with sharp sand. This little charmer of a shrub, which is native to southeastern North America, is worth the effort to meet its requirements. Montrose Nursery offers it, but in limited supply, as it is difficult to propagate.

As for roses, I always round out the year wondering just who Betty Prior is, or was. The single, deep pink rose that is named for her has a remarkable tolerance for neglect, blooming hugely in early June and steadily thereafter right into December most years. It lacks the spectacular tomato-red hips of the rugosas and some of the other species, such as *Rosa moyesii,* but why demand that any plant demonstrate every imaginable virtue? Autumn has its other roses, of course, in a second flush of bloom that is even more welcome than the first one was in June. The cooler nights and the continuing warmth of September days deepen the colors of the flowers without diminishing their fragrance. Like many gardeners

Roses 'Sparrieshoop' (left) and 'Aloha' (right) were both introduced many decades ago, but they remain superior for their persistent bloom over a long season stretching into late autumn, their glossy foliage, and their remarkable fragrance and resistance to disease.

today, I am partial to the older roses, those with names like 'Frau Karl Druschki' and 'New Dawn', rather than those named for Grace Kelly, Cary Grant, and Dolly Parton. If I had more room, I would follow an intriguing suggestion from Vita Sackville-West, who wrote of pegging pillar roses to the ground and training them horizontally as spectacular flowering ground covers.

Finally, to round out this sextet of lingering woodies, there's rose of Sharon, or *Hibiscus syriacus,* but please, not just any old rose of Sharon that turns up. The one to get is the sterile cultivar 'Diana', a fine white with very large blossoms that sidesteps the usual tendencies of the shrub to produce a heavy crop of seeds that can add many hours to late-spring weeding.

As in the old hymn, this porch in Orinda, California, sings "a song of harvest home." The thread-leaf maple is *Acer palmatum dissectum.*

AS WINTER APPROACHES, some woody plants contribute additional interest through the color of their stems, the texture of

their bark, or their form. The stems of kerria and winter jasmine remain a striking green all year round. Yellow-twigged dogwood (*Cornus sericea* 'Flaviramea') strikes me as a bit sickly in color, but red-twigged dogwood (*C. alba* 'Siberica') is splendid. After its leaves fall in November, its stems have a garnet gleam in strong sunlight, and when snow is on the ground, they become especially handsome. The most striking of all late season color, however, comes from the coral-bark maple (*Acer palmatum* 'Sangu Kaku'). This small tree, which stays under ten feet and is hardy to Zone 5, is a deeper pink than coral. "Flamingo pink" says it all. Another maple, the paperbark maple *(A. griseum)* is notable for its attractive, cinnamon-tan, flaking bark. Exfoliating red bark also lends *Lagerstroemia fauriei* great interest in autumn and winter. Hardy to Zone 7, this relative of the crape myrtle *(L. indica),* which produces attractive clusters of white flowers in late summer, is made of sterner stuff than crape myrtles. In the disastrous freeze in the southeastern states in January 1985, which killed many crape myrtles, camellias, and boxwoods to the ground, *L. fauriei* escaped all damage. And for purely sculptural late autumn and winter form, one of my very favorite woody plants is the twisted hazel or "Harry Lauder's Walking Stick" (*Corylus avellana* 'Contorta'). A coarse and uninviting plant in summer, it turns into something purely wonderful once the leaves fall, revealing its wriggling and twisted stems and branches, and the little waxy nubbins of its catkins, which steadily elongate all winter until March, when they reach eight inches long and release their clouds of light gold pollen on the air.

BOTH GARDENERS AND the gardens we make are creatures of time. Wordsworth notwithstanding, once we have passed the first flush of youth and its accompanying illusion that we will go on day after day after day, until the days amount to infinity and eternity, our truest intimations are of mortality, not immortality. Many of the perennials we plant will not long survive us. If we contrive ingeniously to design a garden that makes little or no use of a lawn, we know that the next owner of the house may rip everything out and lay sod. But trees and shrubs are more enduring, and they may

As autumn nears its peak, a garden becomes a place to stroll and to ponder the ever-changing cycle of the seasons. It may also testify to later generations that we were lovers of trees. Who could not love the glowing gold leaves of the ginkgos, which cloak boughs that are raised heavenward?

go on after we have departed to give some testimony to strangers about who we were. The best testimony of all, I think, is that we were lovers—lovers of trees, among some other things. I complain about my swamp maple, its host of seedlings every spring, its greedy robbery of moisture and life-supporting nutrients. But I would not dream of cutting it down, and I will mourn if it goes down in a hurricane, as it came close to doing a few Septembers ago. Someone, a stranger, long gone to earth, planted it perhaps a century ago on the patch of earth we tend, and planted it, I suspect, out of love. It is the last tree in the neighborhood to turn color in the fall. From our bedroom window, when I awaken, I see the progress of pale pink and gold that spreads from the crown, deepening and moving downward with each new morning until, by the end of October, the dawn is aflame with its rich final crimson.

There are trees I have planted on this same piece of property during our tenure here, have planted because I love them. There's that sourwood, for one. For another, there's a dawn redwood *(Metasequoia glyptostroboides).* I planted it partly because it was fast growing, partly because it was a curiosity, a living fossil thought to be long extinct until it turned up in the mid-1940s in a remote part of China. But mostly I planted it because I love the soft and feathery leaves of this deciduous conifer, and their glowing apricot-tan in the autumn, before they fall to form a carpet around the dour green leaves of the hellebores at the base of the tree, which thrive on deep shade in summer and bright, somewhat filtered light in winter.

I don't want to get sentimental or maudlin, and I certainly will not invoke Joyce Kilmer and his poem "Trees," probably the only poem many Americans know by heart. But the plain fact is that trees and other woody plants engage the affections in a powerful way. I defer here momentarily to my friend Joanne Ferguson, writing me early one November about her trip to Princeton, New Jersey, and her return to North Carolina and her shad tree *(Amelanchier canadensis):*

We went to Jersey in mid-October and during the three-day visit, even as we watched, the maples began to flame. It took me back to my New Jersey girlhood from which my most intense memories are of fall and pumpkins and Halloween and red and yellow maples. We came back home to an entirely different world. The tips of the oaks were just beginning to redden. But at that moment the shad tree was perfection. It grows out of the base of a huge white oak, and it wasn't until it made its quiet way up to a second-story bedroom window and covered it with its lacy branches, that I paid it the attention it deserves. Its diameter is no more than six inches, and its blossoms in spring are what is known as insignificant, followed by a few berries to each twig. Its summer color remains a tender spring green. The leaves are no thicker than a few layers of tissue paper, with the result that the pale yellow leaves of fall are translucent. The delicate color is at its best just as the sun is dropping below the horizon, when its unearthly beauty erases quite easily the memory of the gaudy maples. It is rather like the heroine of a nineteenth-century novel, who is thought to be somewhat plain in contrast to the vivid presence of the other characters, until one becomes gradually aware of her fine eyes and quiet grace. The mockingbird eyes us through the window and eats the berries one by one. It's an agreeable sight.

I have no need to plant a shad tree of my own. In her letter Joanne has given me hers, complete with its mockingbird feasting on berries.

Ginkgos are admirable trees, I know. Their fan-shaped leaves are lovely, from their soft green freshness in spring through their yellow gold in autumn. But they have a far greater hold on the affections of some other people I know. One is our younger son, Michael. When he was sixteen, he asked that as a Christmas present we promise to plant a ginkgo in the garden that spring, so we did. He has his own apartment now, but he usually takes a look at the ginkgo when he visits, just to see how it's doing. My friend J. C. Raulston is also a ginkgo man. His knowledge of woody plants in general is vast, and it's clearly a loving kind of knowledge. But it's the ginkgo and its autumn gold that moves him into lyricism, turns him from plant scientist into poet. We had a telephone talk one day. "The color is something almost miraculous," he said, "particularly when a whole street has been planted with nothing but ginkgos. They give a glow to the air like no other plant I know. The light seems to reflect up from the ground, and it is like magic. I sometimes think I would like to buy ten acres of farmland and plant a ginkgo forest there—something that does not exist in nature, since in China these trees have been preserved and saved from extinction by being planted in temple gardens. I can't imagine what it would be like to walk through a two-hundred-year-old stand of these trees, except that I know that the apricot light would make me feel completely and utterly at home on this earth."

Epilogue: In Mid-December

It is a sunny Sunday afternoon, brisk but not chilly enough to need more than a sweater outside, and not yet the time when the cold reaches the bone. The sky is pale, pale blue and quite cloudless. The ornamental grasses have turned to the tan and parchment colors that they will keep most of the winter, except for blue oat grass and Lyme grass, which will hold their slate tints for weeks. The grasses and the white clover in our little patch of lawn still remain a deep and vivid green, but they now have the drama that comes from the long shadows the trunk and branches of our swamp maple cast as the sun becomes ever more southerly, moving toward the winter solstice and the slow rebirth that will follow. The oaks and the sweet gums still hold on to their leaves, but the maples and the sourwoods are bare. The heavy, unlovely leaves of the paulownia tree blackened and fell to the ground weeks ago, in our first light frost. The tree now looks like a great candelabrum. Its branches sweep upward and outward, already bearing the clusters of buds that will open in April into beautiful light purple flowers shaped like slippers and scented of lemon and apricot.

It is winter here now, but the sunlight is still warm and autumnal. The blooming time of the year has not ended . . . and will not end. There are still a few pink flowers on one clump of *Cyclamen hederifolium,* although it is in full leaf now and will not bloom much longer. Nearby, under the more rounded leaves of *C. coum,* the heavy crop of tapered flower buds are almost ready to open. The winter heaths, which showed their fresh buds back in August, have been blooming now for three weeks, a few more every day. The low bushes will be covered with flowers by Christmas. A pink oxalis is still in bloom, and little white flowers, like those of strawberries, have just appeared on a creeping potentilla, *Potentilla tridentata,* ordinarily accounted a spring bloomer. Sweet alyssum keeps on flowering, and its delicate fragrance is still a presence in the garden, like a ghost of summer. A few flowers remain on *Verbena tenuisecta,* now overlain with a metallic sheen induced by chilly nights. Not far away, *V. canadensis,* in several colors, keeps right on blooming. By the kitchen steps, a red annual dianthus is in flower. Next to it, a primrose shows the cardinal-red buds that soon will open. Already blooming is another primrose, deep gold with a large and irregular blotch of apricot on the petals near the throat. I would not have suspected its rich and honeyed fragrance had I not just picked a single blossom for a tiny vase on a kitchen windowsill. In a protected spot against the stone foundation of the house, on the south side for added warmth, and snuggled in amongst a blanket of oak leaves, *Iris unguicularis,* a chancy plant in the northern part of Zone 7, is blooming, just one flower at a time. It will bloom intermittently all through winter, and if the violet-blue flowers are picked before they start to open and are brought indoors, they will develop a sweet scent.

Just as autumn is far from a season of dying, winter is far from a season of death. Life continues. Photosynthesis still takes place in the twigs of maples and other trees, if not at the heady pace of summer, with its warmth and its strong light. In winter, carbon dioxide and sunlight continue to be transformed into the carbohydrates and oxygen on which all life depends. Furthermore, the disappearance of the foliage of deciduous trees and shrubs reveals forms and textures that were concealed during the growing season. The silhouettes of locust trees against the dawn or the twilight sky are hauntingly beautiful. Catalpas, coarse and uninteresting in summer, become exciting in winter, when their long thin pods hang gracefully from their branches. Sycamores, which look trashy and diseased when in leaf, become magnificent in winter for their peeling bark and its complex patterning of white and tan.

Winter is not at all a brown season relieved by the whiteness of snow. Kerrias and winter jasmine remain green, as does the hardy or trifoliate orange *(Poncirus trifoliata),* whose murderous thorns gleam like polished jade to make a lovely sight on mornings when there has been a freezing rain and they are encased in ice. The range of grays is wide. Lambs ears moves from its silver gray of summer to an olive gray. Gray santolinas darken to gunmetal. Most lavenders keep their gray, except 'Jean Davis', which veers toward purple. Woolly thyme holds up well. So does rue: its semiwoody stems may sag slightly, but the blue-gray remains, and it's a fine sight next to aucuba with its bright green leaves spattered with gold.

Nor need winter be without its flowers. Winter jasmine will bloom when a mild spell comes along in January, or when stems are cut and brought inside for forcing. The single, golden-yellow flowers are abundant, and they lift the spirits. Also in January, 'Arnold Promise' and other Chinese hybrid witch hazels will begin their long season of fragrant bloom, almost two months. A few twigs with their wispy flowers are enough to perfume an entire room. In February *Cornus mas,* a wonderful small tree too little planted, will produce its brief but dazzling shower of sulfur-yellow blossoms. The Lenten roses, *Helleborus orientalis,* will start blooming in late February. The subtle color of their bracts—mauve, lavender, creamy white, greenish gray, Joe Pye purple, and combinations of all these colors, with dottings and stipplings and other markings—places them among the true aristocrats of the plant kingdom.

THE DAYS GROW shorter, and the gentle and slanting light of autumn, so welcome after summer's fierce glare and harshness, is departing. Now that the solstice approaches, I will let Elizabeth Lawrence have her say about winter light, for I know of no more telling writing than these words from *Gardens in Winter:*

> The season's beauty is in the quality of the sunlight, which is the more luminous when it is less brilliant, and in the delicacy of the shadows, which are paler and more precise than those of spring or summer or fall. On chance-mild days when an incandescent light falls across gravel walks, my garden seems more beautiful than at any other time. The essence of warmth and light is in this delicate sun that seeps into the spirit and penetrates the marrow. At no other season is the sun so grateful, so gentle, and so healing.

To Miss Lawrence's words and to her sentiments, I can only add Amen.

Sources of Plants

The search for plants appropriate to the late season or autumn garden is sometimes an easy one—as easy as an over-the-fence gift from a neighbor of an especially fine aster or helianthus. But it often does involve searching through the catalogues of mail-order nurseries large or small, all-purpose or highly specialized. What follows is a list of those mail-order nurseries I have either used myself or heard good words about from friends. Some of the catalogues are free, but others cost a small amount—usually $1 or $2—which may be refunded when an order is placed. I have given prices of catalogues, which are, of course, subject to change.

Nurseries come in and out of existence, and in recent years many new ones have sprung up. I expect that this trend will continue in the future. Gardeners have need, therefore, to supplement this list by such means as looking through the classified ads at the back of magazines like *Horticulture, Organic Gardening, Pacific Horticulture,* and others. Word of mouth is also valuable. Two strangers who meet each other and discover that they are both avid gardeners usually lose no time in exchanging praise for their favorite nurseries. (It happens fairly rarely, but sometimes the talk will also turn to misidentified plants or to poor packing.) Another valuable resource for tracking down mail-order nurseries is Barbara Barton's *Gardening by Mail,* which is frequently revised and updated.

Bluestone Perennials, 7211 Middle Ridge Road, Madison, Ohio 44057 (free).

This nursery serves very well the needs of gardeners who don't want to propagate plants themselves, but who are willing to wait for a young plant to reach maturity in their own gardens. Bluestone sells small plants of a very wide range of common perennials at inexpensive prices.

W. Atlee Burpee, 300 Park Avenue, Warminster, Pennsylvania 18974 (free).

Founded in 1875, this mainstay American nursery and seed company has returned to private ownership after some years as part of a large conglomerate. Its several catalogues have a fresh new look, offer valuable advice and meditations on the gardening enterprise, and have become increasingly adventurous in their selection of plants. New company policies support conservation in refusing to sell any bulbs or perennials that may have been collected in the wild.

Canyon Creek Nursery, 3527 Dry Creek Road, Oroville, California 95965 ($2.00).

In its brief history since it was founded in 1985, this nursery has been favored by many discriminating gardeners for its highly personal and slightly offbeat selection of perennials. There is always something in the catalogue, like *Coreopsis rosea* or *Cosmos atrosanguineus,* that isn't available elsewhere. Violas and hardy fuchsias are among the specialties here.

Carroll Gardens, 444 East Main Street, Westminster, Maryland 21157 ($2.00).

This all-purpose nursery sells herbs, roses, and other woody plants, and many choice perennials, including viola 'Molly Sanderson'. Hostas are a specialty, and there is a good assortment of asters.

Crownsville Nursery, 1241 Generals Highway, Crownsville, Maryland 21032 ($2.00).

The catalogue of this small nursery is seldom the same from one year to the next, and there are always a few new plants to try. Quantities are sometimes limited, so placing orders early is advised.

Forestfarm, 990 Tetherhod, Williams, Oregon 97544 ($2.00).

This nursery sells a great many woody plants, some of them rarely offered, in small sizes at inexpensive prices. Gardeners with land to spare can use plants from Forestfarm to establish their own private nursery, growing shrubs and trees in rows until they reach a proper size for landscaping. The emphasis is on western native conifers and deciduous trees and shrubs.

Gossler Farms Nursery, 1200 Weaver Road, Springfield, Oregon 97478 ($1.00).
The specialty here is deciduous magnolias, but autumn-blooming witch hazels and franklinia are also featured.

Heaths & Heathers, P.O. Box 850, Elma, Washington 98541 (SASE).
The name says it all. Several hundred different heaths and heathers are sold wholesale. Retail customers will have to limp along with only two hundred or so to choose among. With a judicious choice of under fifteen plants, gardeners in many parts of the country can have something in bloom every day of the year in colors ranging from white to pink to deep purple. When I visited this nursery one summer, I understood why some people with small gardens plant little else but heathers and heaths and don't feel at all deprived.

Holbrook Farm and Nursery, Route 2, Box 223, Fletcher, North Carolina 28732 ($2.00).
Holbrook is notable not only for its highly personal assortment of perennials and woody plants, but also for its warm and chatty catalogue, often illustrated with humorous and whimsical artwork. The descriptions of plants are based on direct and close observation.

There is always something new and rare.

Huff's Garden Mums, P.O. Box 187, Burlington, Kansas 66839 (free).
This specialty nursery offers an almost paralyzing number of chrysanthemums of many forms and types.

Klehm Nursery, Route 5, Box 197, South Barrington, Illinois 60010 ($2.00).
I give this large nursery, which not only sells retail but is also a wholesale grower for several other well-known mail-order houses, an A + for the quality of its container-grown plants and for the care with which they are packed. Hostas, peonies, irises, and daylilies are all specialties, but Klehm's list of perennials, including autumn bloomers and lingerers, increases every year.

Lamb Nurseries, East 101 Sharp Avenue, Spokane, Washington 99202 (free).
Lamb's tall and skinny catalogue offers a wide selection of perennials. Within each genus, so many cultivars and species are listed that it is hard to say what the nursery's specialties are. There are many sedums and sempervivums, hardy fuchsias, chrysanthemums, asters, and so on, and prices are reasonable.

Logee's Greenhouses, 55 North Street,

Danielson, Connecticut 06239 ($3.00). Logee's sells primarily tender house-plants and greenhouse plants, among them *Mandevilla* 'Alice DuPont', which may be grown as a late season annual vine—or overwintered inside.

Louisiana Nursery, Route 7, Box 43, Opelousas, Louisiana 70570 ($2.00). Gardeners living north of the Mason-Dixon line may be depressed by knowing that some of the plants in this catalogue are not winter hardy, but there is an unusually good selection of liriopes here.

Montrose Nursery, Box 957, Hillsborough, North Carolina 27278 ($2.00).
Considering the role that Nancy Goodwin and Montrose have played in this book, further comment is almost gratuitous. Seed-grown hardy cyclamens are the specialty here, but the list of perennials has grown explosively every year, and it includes many autumn plants—asters in great number, lobelias, salvias, solidaster, *Begonia grandis* (the rare white form as well as the pink), *Patrinia scabiosifolia*, tricyrtis, and some hellebores that will bloom in late fall in the Upper South at least. Catalogue descriptions are detailed and have the accuracy that comes from personal knowledge rather than hearsay.

Niche Gardens, 1111 Dawson Road,

Chapel Hill, North Carolina 27514 ($3.00).
Niche sells primarily North American native perennials that are nursery propagated, not collected in the wild. There is a good selection of native asters and solidagos. The catalogue is one of the few that lists fall-blooming plants separately, dividing them into early fall bloomers and later-flowering ones. Eupatoriums are here in force, including dog-fennel *(Eupatorium capillifolium)*. I reiterate here my suspicion that this truly spectacular perennial may turn out in some gardens to be a gangster.

Park Seed Company, S.C. Highway 254N, Greenwood, South Carolina 29647 (free).
One of the few remaining seed companies that is still owned and operated by the family whose name it bears, Park offers a rich assortment of seeds for both annuals and perennials, as well as a limited number of plants. Its catalogue is one of the first places to look for lablab beans.

Prairie Nursery, P.O. Box 365, Westfield, Wisconsin 53964 ($1.00).
A good source for nursery-grown native grasses and wild flowers of the Midwest.

Sandy Mush Herb Nursery, Route 2, Leicester, North Carolina 28748

($4.00).

I confess to not having tried this nursery—yet—and to the strong temptation to list it strictly for the sake of its name. But several friends swear by it, and the catalogue shows it to have the widest range of ornamental salvias, both tender and winter hardy, in the nursery trade. Its location in the mountains of North Carolina (as with Holbrook and We-Du) means that its plants are adapted to cold winters and are good bets for gardeners in the northern states.

John Scheepers, Inc., RD 6, Phillipsburg Road, Middletown, New York 10940 (free).
Best known for its spring bulbs, Scheepers also sells crocosmias, cannas, and several species of both colchicums and autumn crocuses.

Siskiyou Rare Plant Nursery, 2825 Cummings Road, Medford, Oregon 97501 ($2.00).
The catalogue is a delectable offering of alpine plants in great numbers, some of them late bloomers.

Stokes Seed Company, P.O. Box 548, Buffalo, New York 14240 (free).
Stokes's catalogues have a delightfully old-fashioned flavor, and there are a great many annuals here that have gradually disappeared from other catalogues.

Sunlight Gardens, Route 1, Box 600-A, Andersonville, Tennessee 37705 ($1.00).
Here is another southern nursery with an ecological commitment to propagating its own native plants. Some, such as the lingering blooming purple coneflower, *Rudbeckia tennesseensis*, an endangered species, are grown under permit from the USDA. This is a good source for native species of aster and solidago.

TyTy Plantation, P.O. Box 159, TyTy, Georgia 31795 (free).
TyTy offers many tender subtropical bulbs and perennials at prices reasonable enough that northern gardeners may wish to treat them as annuals. There is a large list of wonderful new cannas that will change the minds of anyone who thinks that cannas are little but relics of the Victorian days of bedding out.

Andre Viette Farm and Nursery, Route 1, Box 16, Fishersville, Virginia 22939 ($2.00).
The specialties here are iris, peonies, hostas, and daylilies, with many of the daylilies being bred by three successive generations of the Viette family. The catalogue also offers a huge assortment of other perennials, including many asters and Japanese anemones. Open to the public during the growing season, Viette's is worth a pilgrimage. On a

hillside in the Shenandoah Valley, within sight of the mountain where John-Boy Walton grew up, the nursery has beautifully designed display beds of herbaceous perennials. Although it does extensive business by mail order, it also sells sturdy and well-established perennials in containers. I have visited often, going light on luggage so there will be room to cram the car with plants on the way home.

Mary Walker Bulb Company, Box 256, Omega, Georgia 31775 (free).
See TyTy Plantation above. The catalogues are remarkably similar.

Wayside Gardens, Hodges, South Carolina 29695 (free).
An all-purpose nursery with a long history, Wayside sells many woody plants as well as herbaceous perennials that are hard to find elsewhere. It is known for its efforts to introduce choice plants of British and European origin. Its huge catalogue, lavishly illustrated with color photographs, has surely been an important element in the education of many an American gardener. Wayside's was the first garden catalogue I ever read, when the nursery was still in Mentor, Ohio, and I was eight years old. Recently, the catalogue has devoted two pages to autumn plants, but many others are described elsewhere in it.

We-Du Nurseries, Route 5, Box 724, Marion, North Carolina 28752 ($1.00). We-Du is a treasure trove for Asiatic woody plants and perennials as well as native North American ones. Its catalogue is short on hype and long on accurate description and temptation.

Well-Sweep Herb Farm, 317 Mount Bethel Road, Port Murray, New Jersey 07865 ($1.00).
This is a good source for many herbs, including both culinary and ornamental salvias.

White Flower Farm, Route 63, Litchfield, Connecticut 06759 ($5.00 for three-catalogue annual subscription).
This institution and its catalogues are to the world of nurseries what *The New Yorker* is to the world of magazine publishing—not surprisingly, since the nursery was originally founded by an editor at the magazine. Good plants, good prose—and another catalogue that has helped educate many gardeners.

Woodlanders, 1128 Colleton Avenue, Aiken, South Carolina 29801 (long SASE).
Woodlanders has a wonderful list of shrubs, trees, and perennials, both native and exotic. Northern gardeners must be sure to order for fall planting, however, since this nursery's spring shipping season ends long before the ice and the snow melt in Connecticut and Minnesota.

Bibliography

Bailey, Liberty Hyde. *The Standard Cyclopedia of Horticulture.* 3 vols. New York: Macmillan, 1933.

Barton, Barbara. *Gardening by Mail.* Third edition. Boston: Houghton Mifflin, 1990.

Blanchan, Neltje. *Nature's Garden.* Toronto: William Briggs, 1900.

Clauson, Ruth Rogers and Nicolas Ekstrom. *Perennials for American Gardens.* New York: Random House, 1989.

Dana, Mrs. William Starr [Frances Theodora Parsons]. *According to Season.* New York: Scribner's, 1894.

————. *How to Know the Wild Flowers.* New York: Scribner's, 1893. Boston: Houghton Mifflin, 1989.

Earle, Alice Morse. *Old Time Gardens.* New York: Macmillan, 1901. Detroit: Singing Tree Press, 1968.

Hardin, James W. and Jay M. Arena. *Human Poisoning from Native and Cultivated Plants.* Second edition. Durham: Duke University Press, 1974.

Harper, Pamela and Frederick McGourty. *Perennials: How to Select Grow, and Enjoy.* Tucson: HP Books, 1985.

Lacey, Stephen. *The Startling Jungle.* Boston: Godine, 1990.

Lawrence, Elizabeth. *Gardening for Love.* Durham: Duke University Press, 1987.

————. *Gardens in Winter.* New York: Harper, 1957.

————. *Lob's Wood.* Cincinnati: Cincinnati Nature Center, 1971.

Lovejoy, Ann. *The Year in Bloom.* Seattle: Sasquatch, 1987.

Rix, Martin and Roger Phillips. *The Bulb Book.* London: Pan, 1982.

Thomas, Graham Stuart. *Perennial Garden Plants.* Revised edition. London: Dent, 1982.

Thoreau, Henry David. "Autumn Tints," in *The Natural History Essays.* Salt Lake City: Peregrine Smith, 1980.

Whittle, Tyler. *The Plant Hunters.* Philadelphia: Chilton, 1971.

Wilder, Louise Beebe. *Adventures with Hardy Bulbs.* New York: Macmillan, 1936.

————. *Colour in my Garden.* New York: Doubleday, 1927. New York: Atlantic Monthly Press, 1990.

————. *The Fragrant Path.* New York: Macmillan, 1932.

Young, Andrew. *A Prospect of Flowers.* London: Jonathan Cape, 1945. New York: Viking, 1985.

Photo Credits

Richard W. Brown: 181, 193

Charles O. Cresson: 143

Edith Eddleman: 41, 74, 111, 113

Nicolas Ekstrom: 176

Nancy Goodwin: 64 (both), 67, 119 (center, right), 127 (center, bottom), 173, 201 (right)

Jerry Harpur: 133, 135

Saxon Holt: 71, 163, 178, 191, 204

Jerry Howard: 91 (left), 166, 195

Allen Lacy: 37 (right), 68–69, 83 (left), 84, 85 (right), 89, 105, 116, 127 (top), 156 (bottom)

Michael Lacy: 114, 122 (left)

Lynden B. Miller: 23, 80 (middle)

John Neubauer: 28, 91 (right), 100–101, 121, 149, 152, 153 (right), 154

Jerry Pavia: 168

Joanna Pavia: 144

Allen Rokach: 7, 24–25, 55, 123, 159, 160, 186

Arty Schronce: 72, 81, 85 (left), 88, 110, 115 (right), 119 (left), 167

Michael S. Thompson: 131, 136, 146, 190

Andre Viette: 60, 80 (left, right), 83 (right), 102, 103, 109 (both), 122 (right), 129

Cynthia Woodyard: ii–iii, 9, 10, 13, 15, 30, 33, 36, 37 (left), 40, 43, 50, 51, 53, 58, 59, 63, 65, 77, 86, 87, 93, 96, 97, 108, 115 (left), 125, 132, 137, 138, 153 (left), 156 (top), 157, 170, 171, 174–175, 187, 189, 194, 197, 201 (left), 202

Index

Boldface page numbers refer to plants mentioned in the photograph captions.